EDUCAR EN VALORES EN LOS ALBORES DEL SIGLO XXI:
PENSAMIENTO ESTÉTICO-FILOSÓFICO Y COMUNICACIÓN

— *Colección Comunicación y Filosofía* —

Educar en valores en los albores del siglo XXI: Pensamiento estético-filosófico y comunicación

Editores

Francisco Javier Escobar Borrego
Lucía Ballesteros Aguayo

Autores
(por orden de aparición)

Francisco Javier Escobar Borrego
Raffaele Lombardi
Gaia Peruzzi
Ana Lucía Murillo Villamar
Hortensia Enriqueta Carranza Rojas
Luis Arboledas Lérida
Tomás Rodríguez Caguana
Guadalupe Vernimmen Aguirre
António Santos Veloso
António Dos Santos Queirós
Oliver Salas Herrera

EGREGIUS
ediciones

EDUCAR EN VALORES EN LOS ALBORES DEL SIGLO XXI: PENSAMIENTO ESTÉTICO-FILOSÓFICO Y COMUNICACIÓN

Ediciones Egregius
www.egregius.es

Diseño de cubierta e interior: Francisco Anaya Benitez

© Los autores

1ª Edición. 2019

ISBN 978-84-17270-89-6

Colección:

Comunicación y Filosofía

Editora científica
Lucía Ballesteros-Aguayo

Editor técnico
Francisco Anaya Benítez

Consejo editorial

Ramón Reig (*Universidad de Sevilla, España*)
Juan Antonio García (*Universidad de Málaga, España*)
Rosalba Mancinas-Chávez (*Universidad de Sevilla, España*)
Manuel Bermúdez (*Universidad de Córdoba, España*)
Eduardo Fernández (*Universidad Autónoma de Chihuahua, México*)
Giovanna Gianturco (*Universidad de La Sapienza, Roma*)
Fernando Figueredo (*Florida International University, USA*)
Gloria Olivia Rodríguez Garay (*U. Autónoma de Ciudad Juárez, México*)
Patricia Álvarez Chávez (*U. Autónoma de Ciudad Juárez, México*)
Marco Fincardi (*Università Ca' Foscari, Italia*)
Juri Meda (*Universidad de Macerata, Italia*)
Giuseppe Ricotta (*Universidad La Sapienza, Italia*)
Jorge Bolaños (*Universidad de Granada, España*)
Alberto Pena Rodríguez (*Universidad de Vigo, España*)
Vania Baldi (*Universidad de Aveiro, Portugal*)
Antonia Isabel Nogales Bocio (*Universidad de Zaragoza, España*)
Juan Francisco Gutiérrez Lozano (*Universidad de Málaga, España*)
Francisco Javier Ruiz del Olmo (*Universidad de Málaga*)

Edita:

EGRÉGIUS
ediciones

ÍNDICE

EDUCAR EN VALORES
EN LOS ALBORES DEL SIGLO XXI:
PENSAMIENTO ESTÉTICO-FILOSÓFICO Y
COMUNICACIÓN

En los albores del siglo XXI se hace bien necesario estimular a las futuras generaciones universitarias para que se decanten por una conciencia responsable y decidida a la hora de *educar en valores*, atendiendo, como un camino edificante y enriquecedor, al binomio *pensamiento estético-filosófico y comunicación*. Para ello, los siete capítulos que articulan el diseño conceptual y arquitectura del presente volumen circunscriben su atención, entre la ciencia y la concepción artística, a la diversidad cultural educativa, las relaciones interdisciplinares y multidisciplinares, la transversalidad y, claro está, las acciones colegiadas y de cooperación orquestadas por variados equipos de investigación procedentes de reconocidos centros académicos de naturaleza y proyección internacional.

En efecto, lo ponen de relieve, en lo que concierne a los progresivos cambios de paradigmas metodológicos europeos y en un maridaje entre ciencias sociales y humanidades, Raffaele Lombardi y Gaia Peruzzi (Sapienza Università di Roma) en *Communication for diversity. An exploratory study on the features of internal communication to manage cultural diversity in the Italian organizations*. A este respecto, se sirven de un encuadre focalizado en el marco conceptual italiano desde el proyecto de investigación *Codes*, gracias a la implicación cooperativa de investigadores procedentes no sólo de Italia sino también de Francia, Alemania, Grecia, Portugal y Rumanía. En esta senda, Ana Lucía Murillo Villamar y Hortensia Enriqueta Carranza Rojas (Universidad Católica Santiago de Guayaquil) proceden, asimismo, mediante un *modus operandi* análogo en *Análisis de la comunicación discursiva en las aulas universitarias ecuatorianas: un resultado de la actual revolución latinoamericana*, pero con el matiz diferencial de que dirigen su mirada y óptica transversal al contexto educativo y de academia universitaria en Hispanoamérica. Por esta razón, siguiendo la estela metodológica de Dussel, optan por el caso específico del sistema educativo reglado en Ecuador al trasluz de paralelismos respecto a otros países hermanados por el prisma sociocultural hispánico como Bolivia, Perú y Chile.

Avanzando en la *economía* discursiva y narratividad analítica de la presente monografía, el lector podrá adentrarse en cuestiones medulares para la eficiente educación en valores en nuestra época. En tan granada labor habrá de tener en cuenta categorías conceptuales tales como el progresivo cambio de paradigmas multidisciplinares, la constante innovación metodológica y de planteamientos epistemológicos hacia la apertura de nuevas perspectivas críticas en la transferencia del conocimiento pero siempre abogando por criterios de rigurosa selección y jerarquía informativa. Ello no es óbice, como refiere Luis Arboledas Lérida (Universidad de Sevilla, Estado español) a propósito de la compañía Tesla como caso de estudio en *Conocimiento científico en acceso abierto y la «mercantilización» de la academia: más allá de la ¿quiebra? del negocio editorial*, para que no tengan cabida la tensión y el debate dialéctico sobre esta renovación de paradigmas; en concreto, en lo que respecta al *open access* de la producción científica y la presumible «mercantilización» fomentada por los sistemas académicos. En otras palabras, tales agentes, al margen de *«paywalls»*, neutralización de coincidencias investigadoras por una deficiente asimilación del estado de la cuestión y hasta un visible rendimiento empresarial, alientan a dicha génesis y transmisión de la comunicación científica pero, con frecuencia, sin la suficiente distancia crítica, como cualquier investigación rigurosa requiere. Por tanto, acaso sea crucial traer a la memoria, en tales tiempos de ritmo y tempo vertiginosos con el objeto de airear publicaciones científicas y artísticas como hojas volanderas, la conocida sugerencia que proponía a sus lectores el poeta romano Horacio, *in illo tempore*, a propósito de dejar pasar una década «prodigiosa»; es decir, guardando y custodiando el original hasta nueve años antes de la revisión definitiva en la *«poetarum limae labor»*, para que la obra, al margen del *«post tenebras spero lucem»*, no permaneciera en las tinieblas antes de que viese la luz, ya desde sus propios cimientos.

En este contexto reticular, con sus luces y sus sombras y no exento de polémica en época de modernidad, industria cultural y miradas poliédricas vinculadas a la intersubjetividad, resulta de sumo interés y vigencia revisar críticamente la función del estado como *ente* y agente implicado en el marco actual de producción capitalista entre la economía, la ciencia y el arte. Para ello se trazan edificantes planteamientos de investigación filosófica, tan importantes en esta época de *deshumanización del arte* y hasta de los valores, en la línea conceptual de los modelos clásicos de la cultura griega, con resonancias y divergencias en Hegel, Schopenhauer, Mattelart, Habermas, Badiou o Žižek, como se trasluce en el capítulo *El Estado capitalista como ente restaurador y comunica-*

cional en las concepciones de Hegel, al cuidado de Tomás Rodríguez Caguana y Guadalupe Vernimmen Aguirre (Universidad de Guayaquil). De hecho, tales cuestiones universales tienden puentes modulatorios con el objeto de brindar renovadas posibilidades de rentabilidad económica desde la transferencia y alta divulgación del conocimiento; baste recordar desde la concepción de los museos virtuales como arte de la memoria, con frecuencia en diálogo con la cultura popular y la oralidad, pasando por variadas y atractivas formalizaciones del turismo, alentadas en virtud de itinerarios y rutas culturales a efectos de patrimonio, hasta llegar, por añadidura, a sutiles implicaciones ecológicas y de sostenibilidad medioambiental. Tanto es así que, cada vez con mayor frecuencia, se está recuperando el prístino *sueño* humanístico, si se quiere, de regresar a la integración primigenia del ser humano con la naturaleza, o sea, a tenor del ideal *vivere secundum naturam*. Lo vienen a exponer detenidamente António Santos Veloso (Centro de formación profesional de profesores de Conimbriga Cefop.Conimbriga I&D) y António dos Santos Queirós (Centro de filosofía de la Universidad de Lisboa CFUL), en *El nuevo paradigma de turismo ambiental y el problema de la comunicación en el turismo*, a partir de paradigmas filosóficos tales como el hedonismo, en calidad de corriente de pensamiento y forma de vida, y el prisma de calado ambientalista, en armonización con el Código mundial de la ética del turismo.

Tales vías de indagación señaladas parten, claro está, de una meditada exploración cualitativa realizada en centros de investigación universitarios, laboratorios y marcos científico-académicos similares, por lo general como fruto del maridaje e imbricación armónica entre la formación teórico-analítica y la creatividad estética. Esto es, por resumirlo de manera sintética, conforme al principio de interdisciplinariedad entre ciencias sociales, humanidades y otros campos al servicio de la investigación, no es de extrañar, en consecuencia, el continuo desarrollo de tecnologías digitales, repositorios y bases de datos afines en el espacio virtual, al tiempo que se viene a apostar, con mayor frecuencia, si cabe, por una educación inclusiva desde el ser auténtico (*self*) como antídoto paliativo contra un palmario egocentrismo narcisista imperante en tales pagos y atalayas privilegiadas de poder; o sea, lejos de discriminación, exclusión y marginación, dogmas teóricos o planteamientos únicos, infalibles y sectarios para cualquier objeto de análisis, por lo general heredados desde una actitud acrítica como patrones anquilosados y limitantes. Son, por tanto, los nuevos objetivos, retos e ideales para el progresivo y alentador avance de la humanidad los siguientes, como el lector irá comprobando a lo largo de estas páginas: pluralidad cultural, etnicidad, *inteligencias múltiples*, igualdad en derechos y oportunidades, libertad y respeto, escucha consciente dirigida a la *alteridad*, género y orientación sexual, ideología, sin marginación o exclusión de personas y de colectivos identitarios, revisión y actualización de los conceptos de transferencia del conocimiento, industria cultural y propiedad intelectual, o, en fin, sensibilidad hacia la ecología, en diálogo con el afecto y protección compasiva hacia los animales.

Pues bien, este último particular, es decir, el de la sensibilización, respeto y responsabilidad orientados hacia el complejo y rico universo de los animales, viene a constituir la coda o *cadenza* final del volumen. De hecho, se identifican dos ópticas e imaginarios diferentes en el tiempo, pero complementarios y al unísono, sobre la necesidad de compromiso cívico-ético por parte del ser humano, tanto a nivel individual como de colectivos socio-culturales, con el objetivo esencial de evitar, paliar y finalmente erradicar el cruel maltrato contra los animales. Y es que tan delicada y espinosa cuestión se hace todavía muy generalizada en época contemporánea, por desgracia, como analiza Oliver Salas Herrera (Universidad de Cádiz) en *Educación sobre los derechos del animal en la serie de animación española «Mofli, el último koala»* (1987). Para ello, este investigador toma como punto de partida y piedra angular dicha serie de animación bajo la rúbrica autorial de Jordi Amorós, en calidad de estudio de caso, y en virtud de una implementación metodológica cualitativa, según el esquema semiológico actancial de Greimas, al trasluz de la Declaración universal de los derechos del animal.

Ahora bien, tan difícil encrucijada, con implicaciones en las emociones y sentimientos complejos del ser a efectos de agresividad, violencia ..., hunde sus raíces, en cuanto a remoto arquetipo, en la psique humana e imaginario colectivo, en términos de Carl Gustav Jung, muy interesado, como es sabido, en las fronteras limítrofes entre la ciencia y la expresión artística. Así lo llegó a plasmar por su parte Cervantes, en las fronteras entre realidad y ficción y desde su poética de la libertad, en un diseño estético-filosófico personal, visiblemente adelantado a su época, que constituyó, a su vez, un modelo genérico-conceptual al servicio de la novela moderna como *puertas del sueño*. De esta manera, si se atiende a una pedagogía *ex contrario*, la exquisita palabra literaria del autor alcalaíno hace copartícipes y cómplices a sus atentos lectores, con mensajes reveladores para los jóvenes de hoy en día, a la hora de sensibilizarlos en el *verosímil* conflicto que plantea a propósito de los animales, reflejo simbólico y ficticio, en definitiva, de las *virtutes et vitia* que se coligen de las acciones cognitivo-conductuales humanas. Así se puede leer al decir de Francisco J. Escobar (Universidad de Sevilla), en *El pensamiento filosófico de Cervantes entre ética y estética (con «mudanzas» y «variaciones» de zarabanda y chacona*) conforme al comparatismo interdisciplinar en la intersección de códigos propuesta entre literatura y música, y con sones coreográfico-musicales como *colonna sonora*. De hecho, según se desvela en las sabrosas páginas de *El Quijote* y *El coloquio de los perros*, se parte, de entrada, de la recepción y reformulación *ejemplar* de la tradición clásica de Apuleyo, con el vocablo *quijote* de fondo en su conocida versión romanceada al castellano desde 1513, auspiciando así *in nuce* el célebre título de la universal novela homónima, si bien están igualmente presentes otros señeros modelos estético-filosóficos del aliento y fuste de Luciano, Séneca, Juvenal y Esopo.

En suma, a la vista de lo expuesto, queda todavía mucho por hacer en el arduo y no fácil proceso de alentar a las nuevas generaciones para que se adentren paulatinamente en la lectura rigurosa y cabal bajo un aprendizaje significativo; sólo de esta manera, se podrá ir forjando en nuestros jóvenes, a veces algunos de ellos un poco bisoños y no demasiado avezados en los «clásicos populares», un pensamiento crítico constructivo entre ética y estética, o lo que es lo mismo, conforme al principio de *educar en valores en los albores del siglo XXI*. Por esta razón, los puentes sutiles y de equilibrio modulatorio entre ciencia y arte, innovación tecnológica y creatividad *humanística* al calor de nuestras raíces fundacionales como *seres en el mundo* acaso constituyan el *recto camino* y la *escondida senda*, como nos ha enseñado fray Luis de León siguiendo las huellas del *secretum iter* horaciano, que hemos de cultivar entre todos en el seno de la comunidad científico-cultural. No obstante, transitando el *pensamiento estético-filosófico* de nuestros más deliciosos referentes clásicos, más allá de tiempos y espacios concretos, sólo así podremos apostar por un mundo solidario, presidido por la libertad pacífica, la igualdad de derechos y la concordia universal; eso sí, utopías, distopías y ucronías al margen, éstos habrán de estar cimentados, en definitiva, por pilares esenciales de la comunicación, ya postulados y propugnados desde la *paideía* y la *humanitas* clásicas, como el respeto, la responsabilidad y el compromiso: *Divinas palabras*.

Francisco J. Escobar
Universidad de Sevilla

COMMUNICATION FOR DIVERSITY.
AN EXPLORATORY STUDY ON THE FEATURES OF INTERNAL COMMUNICATION TO MANAGE CULTURAL DIVERSITY IN THE ITALIAN ORGANIZATIONS

Dr. Raffaele Lombardi
Sapienza University of Rome, Italy

Profa. Dra. Gaia Peruzzi
Sapienza University of Rome, Italy

Abstract

Cultural diversity is one of the distinctive feature of our world. In consequences of a complex intertwining of some deep social processes (secularization and modernization, global media evolutions, international migrations), our societies have become culturally more heterogeneous and fragmented than in the past. These transformations involve all the spheres and institutions, thus also professional organizations.

The management and enhancement of cultural diversity inside organizations and work environments is a topic that in some sense has always being present in the corporate external communication. Indeed, public relations, marketing, advertising are traditionnally interested in intercepting external various categories of stakeholders (*new* customers, buyers, audience, media), so they need to know, understand and handle *continuously new* lifestyles, behaviours, people. In other words, different cultures. But today cultural diversity is emerging also like an internal issue. Especially in medium and large insitutions, corporate world is often characterized by a motley population, that is people with different place and culture of origin, gender, sexual orientation, age, disabilities, family burdens, etc. In the last decades, equal rights and opportunities thought have drawn the attention on the discriminations and disequalities that afflict organizational cultures, giving some inputs to specialized studies and policies. However, these new sensibilities seem to have taken root mainly in Anglo-American and Northern European countries, whereas they are struggling to diffuse in the rest of Europe.

This paper intends to investigate the role that the internal communication can play in promoting and managing the cultural diversity inside the Italian organizations. The difficulties faced by the reserchers in finding case-studies and witnesses available to tell their companies experiences confirm the backwardness of the territory in respect of this issue. Then, this study necessarily is an exploratory research.

The first part of the work is an overview on the current situation in Italy, made on secondary data. We have collected and analayzed the most recent researches on the programmes and experiences made by the Italian public and private organizations to promote cultural diversity.

Next up, the main action is a focus group aimed at exploring how the redefinition of internal relations can promote cultural diversity inside the organization, and the positive effects that an equality-oriented management can have for the life of the company. The focus group involved about ten training and communication managers working in private, public and non-profit Italian organizations.

Finally, it is important to note that the research action presented in this essay is part of a wider European scientific project (Codes, 2017-2019), involving six European countries (France, Germany, Greece, Italy, Portugal, Roumanie). It is focused in a comparative reflection on the relation among cultural diversity, communication and solidarity in our societies, paying particular attention to the educational needs of media, companies, public and no-profit organizations.

Key words

internal communication; cultural diversity; diversity management; discrimination;

1. Multiculturalism, internal communication, diversity management. An introduction

The living together of different pepople and cultures on the same territory is the greatest challenge of the contemporary societies (Giddens, 1994; Kymlicka 1995, Canclini, 1998; Touraine, 2000). Today many countries are a landing place for migrant people, so many territories have to deal with new needs, new identities, new borders, and continuosly emerging questions concerning the overlapping of native and migrant populations, the tensions between the fears of former and new inhabitants, the risks of social inequalities and fractures, and sometimes even the raising xenophobia and racism.

The progressive complexity of societies - due to a series of important processes, such as migration, social emancipation, secularisation - has also affected organizations, with the problem of coexistence between different people and inequality. In some countries this topic has been the subject of study and innovative social policies. Italy began to pay its attention to these issues only in the last years. In literature we begin to talk about managing diversity in professional organizations. If the contemporary society is characterized by people with numerous and important differences therefore also the organizations may be composed by people with different places and cultures of origin, gender, sexual orientation, age, disability, family burdens, etc.

Managing differences in public, private and no-profit organizations is a complex phenomenon because it is closely linked to equal opportunities policies implemented in each country. Organizations are committed to managing diversity through programs that are based on the protection of equal treatment in the workplace and their objective is the employment and depend on national regulatory interventions (De Vita, 2011; Buemi, Conte, Guazzo, 2015).

Diversity management should instead be a strategy of internal communication of organizations. Internal communication, in fact, is dedicated to creating a favorable and inclusive climate and to listening the needs of employees. The aim of diversity management have wider objectives than employment goals. This not only aim to compensate for the disadvantaged elements, but to promote the inclusion of any subject belonging to a minority and therefore not able to exert a power of influence in the organization (Mauri, Visconti, 2004). With the label *diversity management* we mean in fact the set of policies, practices and actions that have the aim of enhancing the diversity of individuals in organizations (Treven, Treven, 2007), interpreting the "diversity" with any difference that involves a "problem" in a given context historical, cultural and social.

The literature review highlights the recent attention of academic professionals to diversity management, especially in Italy. The first reflections date back to the Nineties in the United States (Thomas 1990, Cox, Blake, 1991; Cox, 1993) and a little later the theoretical elaborations spread in Europe, especially in the Anglo-Saxon sphere (Kandola, Fullerton, 1994). In the Italian context, the ideas of international scholars are collected and elaborated in the following years (Barabino et al 2001; Bombelli, 2003). In particular, in 2012 Italian authors formulate a first definition that problematizes the concept of diversity in multicultural society, highlighting the ability to "promote expression of the different predispositions, experiences and identities and to enhance them for the purposes of business performance and the achievement of its objectives" (Monaci, 2012).

In fact the main assumption for the adoption of diversity management is the overcoming of the traditional management model foundid on the homologation of the differences (King et al., 2010), to recognize the enhancement of diversity, in the belief that a "different" work group contributes better to achieving the objectives (Cox, 2001; Hollowell, 2007; Kreitz, 2008).

The management and enhancement of differences in organizations and work environments is a topic that has achieved good interest by Italian professional organizations, especially for the public administrations that, in compliance with the rules against discrimination in the workplace, have activated projects to enhance individual skills and cultural differences among employees. The interest in these issues has certainly activated the function of external communication in the organizations. Public relations, marketing, advertising are sectors that have long been interested in communication, especially to intercept external stakeholders (Gibson, 2002; Tuleja, 2016).

External communication strategies have adapted languages and tools to the needs of a multicultural society, which must be able to speak to different people respecting the peculiarities of each category of consumers. For a long time, public, private and non-profit organizations have begun to reflect on the use of images in advertising and on the inclusion to no-traditional organizational forms (as in the case of concept of "family").

Today the multicultural issue is not only in reference to consumers and users, but also to the internal workers inside the organizations. The differences can often become problematic inequalities that are reflected in the relational sphere of organizations. The multicultural issue began an important topic also for the internal communication and not only for advertising and external relations. Internal communication is the set of information, communication and training activities addressed at the organizational community. The important feature, as is known, it is the triple function - informing, communicating, training - supporting the engagement of people and the creation of a cohesive and inclusive organizational climate (Cowan, 2017; Mishra et al., 2014).

Multicultural diversity has become a structural feature in our society. Whether it is considered to be of an ethnic/cultural, generational, gender, personality (classifiable, therefore, as *primary diversity*), or that includes elements that can be acquired over time such as professional training or belonging to organizational cultures (*secondary diversity*), ignoring their existence would mean not understanding the reality that can be found in the everyday life of every individual (Olsen, Martins, 2012; Konrad, Prasad, Pringle, 2006).

Even organizations, public, private or no-profit, are affected by this change of paradigm: in fact, until a few years ago it was possible to find, within an organization, a limited level of diversity, at least from the point of view ethnic/cultural (Preeti, 2014; Ahmed, Swan, 2006). Today the situation has radically changed, also thanks to various processes in progress such as the globalization and the internationalization of markets, the need to relate with different stakeholders, new migration processes.

The concept of multicultural organization is closely linked to "multicultural capital" that can be defined as the *set of distinctive cultural features* of an organization. This features represent the intangible "assets" that determine the nature of the organization. Some of the typical elements that make up the cultural asset of an organization are: the values actually shared; the organizational paradigms; the practices associated with creative processes and innovation; the way to deal with situations; the way of conceiving relationships inside and outside the organization (Olsen, Martins, 2012).

2. Research objectives and method

The purpose of this essay is twofold.

Firstly, we propose a review of the most recent Italian letterature on the subject of diversity management to investigate the awareness of the national companies and institutions about the multicultural evolution of their corporate worlds. Indeed, we identified the approach of the diversity management like a key entry to explore the change of the internal communication in front of the progressive differentiation of their population, and the attitude of the companies to activate projects specifically aimed at promoting diversity. This first part of the work is based on secondary data analysis. In absence of official national census of the internal population of companies living on the peninsula, the authors have collected the reports made by the most important industry, public and private organizations. In detail, our source were the following: the data collected by the National Anti-Discrimination Office, for the public sector; the researches of the DiversityLab of Bocconi University, concerning the small and medium enterprises, that is the most diffused model of organization in Italy; then, the data collected by CSVnet, the National Voluntary Services Network, on the internal composition of voluntary associations.

After this preliminary action, the main goal of the research was to investigate how news strategies of internal communication, inspired to the approach of diversity management, can improve the internal wellness of the organization, and, so, its productivity. In other words, we focussed on the processes activated by some "enlightened" governance to promote the ackwoledgement of different needs inside organization, and on the positive effects that an equality-oriented management can have for the life of the entire company.

In this second part of the work, we conducted a focus group interviews involving the communication and personnel managers of some Italian private, public and no-profit organizations. The group was made by about ten people, individuated by a careful selection process, taking into account the following criteria.

Firstly, these managers had to have demostrated an interest in communication of the social problems, understood as "the whole of those communication activities carried out with the intention of increasing humanitarian and solidarity relations among people, the cohesion and wellness of the community» (Peruzzi, 2011). In practice, they have a sound experience in facing issues concerning different kinds of discrimination in the work environments, or better directly in doing diversity management projects. Then, they were women and men, working in many companies and associations, living various organizational cultures, coming from different Italian regions.

Operationally, the focus has been set along the line of a low directivity and a low level of structuring of the discussion track, where the researchers have limited ourselves to create a series of stimulus questions. Indeed, according to the exploratory nature of this study, the aim of this focus group was to give as ample as possible space to the interviewees to freely expose their opinions, and to encourage the exchange of ideas. The expected output was a dense tissue of tells and ideas, expressing the needs of each organization, and supporting the operation of an intersubjective construction of meanings, that is the peculiar characteristic of the focus group (Colella, 2011).

3. Experiences and policies on diversity management in the Italian organizations

The photograph of the diversity in the Italian organizations is monitored by national surveys, that describe the plural composition of organizations. However, these researches do not gives a census of the *policies* for the management and enhancement of differences.

In the public sector, even if we can not speak of a real national monitoring, there is a review of the best experiences in the public administration which have adopted the principles required by the European Commission (Buemi, Conte, Guazzo, 2015).

The European Commission has recognized the role of the European Diversity Charters in helping to hinder discrimination in workplace and promoting equity. Financing the European Platform of Diversity Charters since 2010, Italy has published the "Charter for equal opportunities and equality at work", voluntarily signed by organizations for the dissemination of a corporate culture and inclusive human resources policies.

In the private sector, the most reliable photography on diversity management initiatives is given by the Diversity Management Lab which, since 1999 within the SDA Bocconi, highlights a certain backwardness of organizations in the adoption of policies for diversity. From the data collected on 150 company executives with over 250 employees, it emerges that only 21% said they had adopted policies for diversity (Diversity Management Lab, 2016). This concept is applied almost exclusively to the issue of gender equality and the management of older workers.

The result is that diversity is declined exclusively in two areas and there is no specific attention to other differences. Organizations that want to sensitize their employees in order to create an inclusive and cohesive climate must necessarily start a self-reflection on the internal differences and on the possibility that these differences may create relational problems.

To start a process of self-reflection it is important first of all recognize the importance of the issue and identify a professional figure to train top management and to transmit values and behavior. The human resources managers interviewed do not have a clear idea about the concept of diversity. The 76% of executives respond in a "generic way" without describing concrete cases of application and the 5% of respondents are unable to provide any definition of diversity.

The most controversial element is that about a third of respondents (29%) are not interested in adopting iniciatives to manage cultural diversity that, in any case, are declined in 80% of cases in "practices and strategies to ensure the selection process and the career staff ", and not to affect the culture and behavior within the organization (Diversity Management Lab, 2016).

Finally, the data on the private sector also show that with the increase in the number of women in the labor market there is a different gender distribution in the business sectors as well as in the organizational hierarchies (Saraceno, 2008; Cuomo, Mapelli, 2012; Istat, 2015) and, even more, in the gender pay gap (Istat, 2016).

If we analyze only the large companies, the result elaborated by the Diversity Management Lab changes significantly: the focus of diversity in terms of gender and age is considerably wider because the companies have economic resources to be allocated to this cause. For examples: Carire-Cassa di Risparmio of Reggio Emilia in order to maternity programs; IBM for the enhancement of the skills of the disabled; Feltrinelli in partnership with the Municipality of Milan to supporting workers of foreign origin; Eli Lilly for the extension of corporate benefits to homosexual couples and families.

During the last Diversity Brand Summit (Milan, 2018) they were presented the results of the Diversity Brand Index research, demonstrating that the Italian population prefers the inclusive brands and that attention to strategies for diversity leads to an acceleration of growth (+ 16.7%; Focus Management SpA, Diversity, 2017). Through the Diversity Brand Award, the first European event that connects diversity with international brands, they have been awarded the best inclusives companies and at the top of the ranking there are only large companies: Coca-Cola, American Express, Google, Tim and Vodafone.

The list of Italian companies "promoted" by consumers in terms of diversity, as well as the best practices highlighted by the several European project (for examples DyMove) reinforce the idea that small and medium businesses can not reproduce the experiences and tools of diversity management matured in big business and large companies. In organizational contexts where managerial levels are not high, it is necessary to re-think a model for the promotion of diversity, otherwise the rates of adoption of these policies will remain low or, in any case, only the great enterprise that, in Italy, represents a small portion of the market.

Our analysis of secondary data and the collection of significant research experiences on policies for diversity also concerned the Italian Third Sector. From the IX Census of Industry and Services and Non-Profit Institutions (Istat, 2011), significant problems persist due to the lack of presence of women and young people in the roles of responsibility and the almost total absence of non-EU citizens in the no profit sector. According to the most recent National Report on Voluntary Organizations (CSVnet, 2015), the legal representation of organizations are men in two-thirds of the cases investigated.

Examining the most important voluntary associations (Avis, Anpas, Cives Onlus, Italian Red Cross) most of the managers are men. The same critical issues also emerge in relation to: prevalence of people between 55 and 64 y.o.; participation of subjects belonging to wealthy families (23.4%) against those with insufficient resources (9.7%); episodic involvement of non-EU citizens (3, 54%).

4. The role of internal communication on diversity management

Internal communication means the set of business communication activities aimed at creating an internal network of information flows to disseminate information and knowledge to its employees.

The highly strategic value of internal communication is to consider aspects such as the quality of life in the workplace, the identity and the sharing of objectives, the ability of employees to become ambassadors of the organizations. The three functions mentioned in the introduction of the essay – to inform, to communicate, to train - allow us to understand that priority is not only the circulation of messages (informing) but also the engagement of people (communicating and training) to improve the environment of work.

More generally, the first beneficiaries of a winning internal communication are the company's know-how and the efficiency of its structures and its production processes, the solidity of the corporate culture and, last but not least, the talents of the individual.

The goal of the focus group was to understand if the organizations had started a process of self-reflection on cultural diversity and how manage the internal differences. We conduct a explorative brainstorming through the meeting of special witnesses, all experts in communication, coming from the world of public, private and non-profit organizations.

In the previous paragraph, we have seen that diversity management initiatives are not very widespread in our organizations and, even worse, the positive experiences are not adequately communicated, either within or outside organizations.

The interviews were built with the aim of understanding the difficulties of corporate communications manager in the recognition and enhancement of differences.

The results allow to identify at least two relevant issues. The first one of a managerial nature refers to the organizational hierarchy and the internal communication function. The second one, instead, refers to an essentially cultural and language problem. Compared to the first element, the experts interviewed agree that the greatest difficulty in implementing policies for diversity lies in the approved composition of top management.

> «Companies can not understand and manage diversity if the management groups are effectively homogeneous. Those who select workers tend to reproduce that homologation and are not culturally prepared to value diversity».

In fact, the data presented in the previous paragraph confirm this element. The tendency to perpetuate homologation is an important risk factor and can not be defeated if the top management is homologated. The consequence of this approval is also evident in the structure of the organization. The operational units (offices, divisions, sectors) dedicated to cultural diversity do not operate across the whole organization but are part of the Marketing function. According to the respondents this decision is due to a "perspective error" in internal communication:

> «We often talk about diversity and communication exclusively with reference to the outside world. The diversity that affects companies is that of consumers and citizens and therefore becomes an issue of marketing, advertising, public relations and external communication».

All the positive experiences of exploiting the differences mentioned by the interviewees are related to projects addressed to users/consumers/citizens. When asked to turn their attention within the organization, the examples were limited to the selection process and career strategies. The corporate function dedicated to communication is concerned with the issue of diversity exclusively in the incoming process and not during the working life of people. The true element of innovation does not lie in the "incoming selection processes", but in the ongoing enhancement programs.

This element is linked to a second critical aspect that emerged during the discussion with the experts: *the overly informative nature of internal communication*. The internal communication may be not limited to inform and to disseminate, but must have an impact on the sense of participation and involvement of employees.

The most cited practice among stakeholders was to encourage the emergence of bottom-up participation. In other words, to allow the transmission of skills and knowledge, there must first be an open channel between the higher organs of the organizations and the lower levels. Dialogue, however, should not be seen only as an opportunity to listen, but primarily as a bridge to start inclusive actions.

> «The organizational culture must not therefore be transmitted to workers and members, but must be the fruit of a common effort and must continually reposition itself to adapt to changing times».

This process of inclusiveness is therefore the sum of many conscious efforts. The biggest lack noticed by the experts who are called by companies to talk about managing diversity is the absence of a well-defined flow chart. Given the increasing specialization of each individual's tasks, few workers at low levels know the actual flow of their work and the chain of command configuration. The absence of clear information on the position occupied by each employee, on their contribution compared to the work carried out overall by the organization, generates a low perception of inclusiveness within the company processes that often leads to a lack of participation in the cultural and value environment.

According to the focus group participants the understanding of the working environment is essential for every diversity management activities that are based on the contextual reality of the organization.

The second issue emerged during the group discussion among the interviewed professionals emphasizes a cultural resistance from the organizations.:

> «The meeting with diversity has a problem of language: people do not know which words to use, they do not have a "vocabulary of acceptance and tolerance". For fear of discriminating, organizations often prefer to be silent. And in this way, distance and discrimination increase».

This second cultural aspect leads to the same conclusion of the reflection made in relation to the first critical element, the management one. That is to say that the most powerful weapon possessed today by organizations is education and training. The problem of language and, therefore, the lack of knowledge of the different becomes more and more an emergency in a context that stigmatizes discrimination by law. The interviewees say that in organizations some differences are silenced because people do not have the tools (language, knowledge, experience) to deal with the speech. They do not know how to name certain situations and to avoid relying on clichés and stereotypes they prefer not to take part in the discussion.

However, the absence of specific training within organizations does not encourage dialogue among employees, does not stimulate mutual knowledge and, consequently, accentuates the phenomenon of marginalization of the different.

These are policies that aim to spread the need to understand diversity no longer with a negative meaning, therefore as something to avoid or isolate because it is far from "normal", but on the contrary as something to be valued and appreciated because in it it contains the true essence of being unique.

5. Conclusive reflections and future perspectives

The problem highlighted at the beginning of the essay is the scarce attention of organizations to a self-reflection on internal cultural diversity. Alongside the review of the main scientific contributions, the experiences of concrete application gathered through the research actions mentioned above, bring out at least two important difficulties.

On the one hand, it is decidedly simpler, almost natural, to reproduce the homogeneity of the workforce, rather than to promote its heterogeneity, which implies a cognitive effort and a cultural change on the part of top management, heir to a formation less attentive to an education for multiculturalism.

On the other hand, a theory of diversity management is difficult to generalize precisely because of intervening variables both at the macro level (national legislation) and at the micro level (the specific organization, the socio-cultural environment and productive sector).

The communication strategies are based more on the differentiation of consusers and the construction of a differentiated work environment depends on the assessment procedures that often do not problematize the differentiation of the working group (Cuomo, Mapelli, 2007; Romanenko, 2012).

The reconstruction of the panorama of policies and experiences dedicated to cultural diversity and the listening to privileged witnesses shows some peculiarities of the Italian context: the absence of systematic national monitoring makes believe that they are completely absent in professional organizations, while often it is problem of internal communication and promotion of the same, resulting also to a weak attention from the scholars; on the other hand, the Italian economic-entrepreneurial context is largely made up of small and medium-sized companies, often family-owned. This last element is fundamental to understand the sensitive distance between Italy and other European countries characterized by "large companies" internationalized. It is no coincidence that Italian diversity management experiences are limited to large companies or multinational groups.

In fact, the two elements that emerged from the dialogue with professionals are particularly interesting for two reasons. First of all, both management and cultural issue leverage on a specific need: the fundamental role of systematic training that intervenes on the management side (organization chart and company functions) and on the cultural side of the employees. In the second instance, they highlight the need to give a priority role to internal communication, as an engine for the development of the corporate culture and a tool for mutual knowledge, acceptance and enhancement of diversity (Peruzzi, Lombardi, 2018).

Recognizing and promoting different identities into the organizations, support the redefinition of internal relations in order to stimulate creativity, adaptability and flexibility in front of new and unforeseen situations; but also reduce discrimination and implement the ability for mediation and negotiation of conflicts within organization. So, the future for research in this issue must go in the direction of understanding which internal differences create a problem into the organizations and what problems they create for productivity. Only in this way, the management of diversity begin a form of inclusive management, so as not to continually exclude new forms of diversity.

In this scenario it will be interesting to continue monitoring the role of internal communication, not only as a means to convey information, but as a structural and strategic factor for the life of the organization. The shift from communicative models (top-down), to conversational and then pragmatic/performative models put emphasis on horizontal interactions and non-verbal forms of communication. If the paradigm shift is really shared by the community (the specific organization but, may be, also the Nation), the prospects for the *communication for diversity* have good potential, also taking advantage of the opportunities offered by new media and technologies.

Bibliographic references

Ahmed S., Swan E. (2006). Doing Diversity. Policy Futures in Education, 4, 2, pp. 96-100.

Barabino M.C., Jacobs B., Maggio M.A. (2001). Il Diversity Management, Sviluppo e Organizzazione, 184, pp. 19-31.

Beck U. (2009). Che cos'è la globalizzazione. Rischi e prospettive della società planetaria. Bologna: il Mulino.

Bombelli M.C. (2003). Uguali o diversi? Riflessioni per un utilizzo consapevole del Diversity Management. Economia e Management, 5, pp. 99-110.

Buemi M., Conte M., Guazzo G. (a cura di) (2015). Il Diversity Management per una crescita inclusiva. Strategie e strumenti. Milano: Franco Angeli.

Canclini N.G. (1998). Culture ibride. Strategie per entrare e uscire dalla modernità. Milano: Guerini e Associati.

Colella F. (2011). Focus group. Ricerca sociale e strategie applicative. Milano: Franco Angeli.

Cowan D. (2017). Strategic Internal Communication: How to Build Employee Engagement and Performance. London: Kogan Page Ltd.

Cox T. (1993). Cultural Diversity in Organizations. Theory, Research and Practice. San Francisco: Berrett-Koehler.

Cox T. (2001), Creating the Multicultural Organization. A Strategy for Capturing the Power of Diversity, Jossey-Bass, San Francisco.

Cox T. Jr., Blake S. (1991), "Managing cultural diversity: implication for organizational competitiveness", Academy of Management Executuve, 5, 3, pp. 45-56.

CSVnet (2015). Report Nazionale sulle Organizzazioni di Volontariato. Roma: Fondazione IBM Italia.

Cuomo S., Mapelli A. (2007). Diversity Management. Gestire e valorizzare le differenze individuali nell'organizzazione che cambia. Milano: Guerini e Associati.

Cuomo S., Mapelli A. (2012), Un posto in CDA. Costruire valore attraverso la diversità di genere, Egea, Milano.

De Vita L. (2011). Il Diversity Management in Europa e in Italia. L'esperienza delle Carte della diversità. Milano: Franco Angeli.

Diversity Management Lab (2016). Mappare, condividere, agire. Milano: SDA Bocconi School of Management.

Focus Management S.p.A., Diversity (2017). Diversity Brand Index. Milano.

Gibson R. (2002). Intercultural Business Communication: An Introduction to the Theory and Practice of Intercultural Business Communication for Teachers, Language Trainers, and Business People. Oxford: OUP.

Giddens A. (1994). Le conseguenze della modernità: fiducia e rischio, sicurezza e pericolo. Bologna: il Mulino.

Hollowell B.J. (2007). Examining The Relationship Between Diversity And Firm performance. Journal of Diversity Management, 2, 2, pp. 51-60.

Istat (2011). IX Censimento dell'Industria e dei Servizi e delle Istituzioni no profit. Roma.

Istat (2015). Indagine sulle discriminazioni in base al genere, all'orientamento sessuale e all'appartenenza etnica. Roma.

Istat (2016). I differenziali retributivi nel settore privato-anno 2014. Roma.

Kandola R.S., Fullerton J. (1998). Diversity in Action: Managing the Mosaic. London: CIPD.

King E.B., Gulick L.M.V., Avery D.R. (2010). The Divide Between Diversity Training and Diversity Education: Integrating Best Practices. Journal of Management Education. 34, 6, pp. 891-906.

Konrad A., Prasad P., Pringle J. (2006). Handbook of workplace diversity. London: Sage.

Kreitz P. (2008). Best Practices for Managing Organizational Diversity. The Journal of Academic Librarianship, 34, 2, pp. 101-120.

Kymlicka W. (1995). Multicultural Citizenship. Oxford: Oxford University Press.

Mauri L., Visconti L.M. (2004). Diversity Management e società multiculturale. Milano: Franco Angeli.

Mishra k., Boynton L., Mishra A. (2014). Driving Employee Engagement: The Expanded Role of Internal Communications. International Journal of Business Communication, 51, 2, pp. 183-202.

Monaci M. (2012). Culture nella diversità, cultura della diversità. Una ricognizione nel mondo d'impresa. Milano: Franco Angeli.

Olsen J.E., Martins L.L. (2012). Understanding organizational diversity management programs: A theoretical framework and directions for future research. Journal of Organizational Behavior, 33, pp. 1168–1187.

Peruzzi G., Lombardi R. (2018). Un nuovo attore nel sistema della formazione nazionale: il Terzo Settore e l'esperienza del progetto Formazione Quadri del Terzo Settore del Sud Italia. Scuola Democratica, 2, pp. 335-355.

Peruzzi, G. (2011). Fondamenti di comunicazione sociale. Roma: Carocci.

Preeti B. (2014). Workforce Diversity Management: Biggest Challenge Or Opportunity For 21st Century Organizations. Journal of Business and Management, 16,4, pp.102-107.

Romanenko A. (2012). Cultural diversity management in the organizations. The role of phsycological variables in diversity initiatives. Hamburg: Diplomica Verlag GmbH.

Saraceno C. (2008). Tra uguaglianza e differenza. Il dilemma irrisolto della cittadinanza delle donne, Lettura annuale Ermanno Gorrieri, Modena.

Thomas R.R. (1990), "From Affirmative Action to Affirming Diversity", Harvard Business Review, 68, pp. 107-17.

Touraine A. (2000). Can W Live Together? Equality and Difference. Stanford: Stanford University Press.

Treven S., Treven U. (2007). Training in Diversity Management. Journal of Diversity Management, 1, 2, pp. 29-36.

Tuleja E.A. (2016). Intercultural Communication for Global Business: How leaders communicate for success. London: Routledge.

ANÁLISIS DE LA COMUNICACIÓN DISCURSIVA EN LAS AULAS UNIVERSITARIAS ECUATORIANAS: UN RESULTADO DE LA ACTUAL REVOLUCIÓN LATINOAMERICANA

Mgs. Ana Lucía Murillo Villamar
Universidad Católica Santiago de Guayaquil

Dra. Hortensia Enriqueta Carranza Rojas
Universidad Católica Santiago de Guayaquil

Resumen

La comunicación que actualmente la academia universitaria desarrolla en las aulas, inicia desde el discurso difundido en algunos países de América Latina como Bolivia, Perú, Chile y Ecuador. No obstante, desde hace más de una década, la práctica establece un argumento inconsistente induciendo al caos y la confusión acerca de lo que debemos ser y hacer para incluir estos conocimientos en el pensamiento colectivo. A partir de la mirada de Dussel (2016), proponente de una revolución descolonizadora del pensamiento, se fija este estudio en lo discursivo y no las intervenciones o casos que se auto inscriban en la acción social de la educación con el fin de reflexionar desde la perspectiva descolonizante sobre la producción epistemológica que el mensaje contemporáneo consigue a través de la intervención académica en las jóvenes mentes. Pensar la metodología cimentada en el enfoque cualitativo ha incluido la revisión de teorías representativas sobre propuestas educativas nacionales y su declaración a través de los discursos en las aulas del Ecuador, para este caso universitarias. Asimismo la interdisciplinariedad en el contexto de las ciencias sociales que sustentan el análisis de los indicadores contenidos en el tema de estudio. La operacionalización de conceptos desde su propia naturaleza, apuesta por el método que da cuenta de los fenómenos sociales con mayor pertinencia de estudio, con la intención de clarificar ideas que orienten a la construcción de una praxis fundamentada en la teoría de la descolonización del pensamiento. Desde de este punto, se discuten las limitaciones y perspectivas de desarrollo educativo que fomente o no el pensamiento independiente para ubicarse realmente como una nación multiétnica y pluricultural.

Palabras Clave

Comunicación, educación, descolonización, cultura, discursos, universidad ecuatoriana.

1. **La base del discurso académico sudamericano.**

La globalización que hoy nos envuelve, ansía por reaprender de aquella instrucción por la cual restituir el equilibrio, proteger, preservar y ser parte de un sistema en el que el hombre es un ente más, como una premisa impostergable recordada en los derechos colectivos ancestrales, reconocidos internacionalmente en el Convenio 169 de la Organización Internacional del Trabajo – OIT.

"Nuestra sabiduría ancestral nos enseña que debemos caminar hacia adelante, pero siempre mirando hacia atrás para nunca olvidar lo que somos y así proyectar nuestro futuro" señalaba Evo Morales, citando un fragmento de la cosmovisión andina Abya Yala, durante una conferencia de prensa ofrecida el 26 de marzo frente a la puerta del Palacio de La Paz en La Haya. Esta mirada que plantó el empeño de Sudamérica por reivindicar su historia, sus costumbres y prácticas ancestrales, hizo que en pleno siglo XXI, se escucharan nuevas voces en proyectos de gobierno (Bolivia, Ecuador y Venezuela), y movimientos sociales e indigenistas, reclamando con más fuerzas que antes de la presencia y el respeto de los saberes y las culturas con esencia originaria en el contexto general.

Vivir la vida en toda su plenitud, desarrollarse integralmente, disfrutar de lo que está al alcance y de lo mejor que nos brinda la Madre Naturaleza, vivir en armonía consigo mismo, entre otros aspectos, es la percepción del Buen Vivir, que aunque identificada en todas nuestras culturas de partida con un vocablo diferente (UtzK'aslemal – JelikK'aslemal, Pueblo Maya; K'iche, Guatemala; SumakKawsay, Pueblo Quechua, Ecuador; Suma Qamaña, Pueblo Aymara, Bolivia; ÑandeReko, Pueblo Guaraní, Bolivia; Jlekilaltik, Pueblo Tojolabal, México; Lekilkuxlejal, Pueblo Tzeltal, México) representa un significado análogo que conviene ser leído como una filosofía de vida, como una moral. Expresión que rige toda una cosmogonía que hoy más que nunca puede y debe convertirse en una plataforma axiológica/conductual, ética y estética desde la cual hacer frente al derroche, la depredación, la injusticia social, el desequilibrio y el consumismo que están socavando el hogar natural de la especie humana.

Desde lo comunicológico/interdisciplinar se anhela una nueva lectura de las posibles apropiaciones que en lo cultural, y sobre todo en el campo de la comunicación pública fortalecerían cosmovisiones y levantarían al lugar que merecen las fiestas, las creencias y las leyendas tradicionales, como principal conocimiento. Esto significa resituar las prácticas de derechos, la convivencia social y cultural de nuestras tierras, no solo extendiendo su importancia en el callejón interandino, espacio donde se ha mantenido fuertemente a pesar de la homogenizante información, sino en todos los territorios del continente que apuesten por una renovación de políticas gubernamentales, proyectos nacionales y nuevas leyes que compartan lo mejor de las tendencias socialistas, involucrando a los sectores comprometidos con el bienestar nacional.

En el Ecuador, en cuya constitución (2008) se refrenda su condición de república multiétnica y pluricultural, se vive un proceso intenso de democratización política. Programas de gobierno como el Plan Nacional para el Desarrollo del Buen Vivir, buscan subvertir esquemas y paradigmas de producción y consumo que no responden a las verdaderas esencialidades de nuestra gente. Al mismo tiempo, a través de estos programas, se intenta reivindicar el rescate y la difusión de los saberes ancestrales.

A partir de los lineamientos constitucionales, la regulación de los medios de comunicación, da cabida a espacios democráticos entre medios privados y públicos con una propensión hacia la Educomunicación[1], que desde el 2011 se difundiera con el proyecto de Teleducación[2] (televisión educativa), como estrategia para la actualización y fortalecimiento de currículos de la educación básica general, el nivel de bachillerato y la construcción del currículo unificado de educación inicial en afán de mejorar la calidad y equidad de la persona, implementar un sistema nacional de evaluación, y revalorizar la profesión docente, alineada a intenciones como la propuesta boliviana que se replicaron en el resto de los países del continente sudamericano.

Sin embargo, a pesar de las excelentes intenciones por una sociedad ecuatoriana más propia de su territorio y sus orígenes, sostenemos principios eurocéntricos en las líneas curriculares educativas que lejos de impulsar estudios que dignifiquen culturalmente lo que tenemos, han creado ligeras divergencias acerca de lo que debemos ser o lo que debemos hacer para el fortalecimiento identitario. Sin una lúcida idea de lo que conlleva la propuesta de revalorización cultural y su connotación, los futuros estudios e indagaciones se perfilan incompletos, integrantes de un ciclo de enseñanza-aprendizaje con visiones distorsionadas del sistema significativo de sus términos, razón por la cual, la rendición investigativa de la academia hasta este momento resume la importancia del legado identitario a un ameno visibilizar de danzas y

---

[1] Se define la Educomunicación como una propuesta democrática educativa que interviene haciendo uso de los medios de comunicación.

[2] Puede revisarse información adicional en esta dirección gubernamental. https://educacion.gob.ec/wp-content/uploads/downloads/2015/11/Proyecto_Teleeducacion1.pdf

canturreos, rituales andinos que aunque llenos de valor ancestral solo son admirados por su colorida vistosidad, su creativa apariencia y sus exóticos[3] movimientos.

El filósofo y educador argentino Enrique Dussel asocia estas recurrentes y explosivas difusiones de prácticas andinas con una atadura mental colonizada, un intento fallido de manifestación liberadora de los aprendizajes exclusivamente extranjeros que forman parte del relato contemporáneo en las aulas latinoamericanas. Los mismos espacios en donde se habla de revolución, de independencia, de identidad, de libertad, de autonomía, son los mismo espacios que reproducen de manera mecánica lo andino, por lo tanto, sin educación que rompa la exterioridad, insistente y clamadora por un replanteamiento de los estatutos formativos en todos los niveles para la "transformación de la educación hacia la descolonización de la pedagogía" (Dussel, 2018), lo que respondería a algunas de las incoherentes menciones que en espacios políticos se escudan tras las líneas constitucionales.

> ...el pensamiento crítico debe dar un horizonte de largo plazo, pues una revolución que no llega a una descolonización del pensamiento, sigue siendo colonial.
>
> Debemos tomar conciencia de qué tenemos en la cabeza, en el fondo, una interpretación eurocéntrica de todo,...Debemos entender que el último nivel de la dominación, y al mismo tiempo de la transformación histórica, es una cierta visión del mundo... Tenemos que ver que nuestro mundo latinoamericano, el que tenemos por delante, es colonial... Y el mismo pueblo a veces,...tal es la influencia de la educación, de los medios de comunicación, de la televisión, que llega a despreciarse a sí mismo y anhela salir. No podrá hacerlo, tendrá que aprender a revalorizar lo propio y a partir de allí construir un proyecto de felicidad (Dussel, 2016).

Desde la propuesta de Dussel hace falta una revolución descolonizadora de pensamiento que permita hacernos cargo del presente y responsables de nuestra participación académica, tratando de, en el caso de Ecuador, organizar el discurso que desde la mirada arqueológica europeizada se nos ha brindado sobre la cultura, reversionando los conocimientos adquiridos con las ya frecuentes indagaciones realizadas en

---

[3] Término utilizado para este momento que se presume expresar desde la percepción de las autoras, el poco alcance que tiene el reconocimiento hacia lo ancestral, haciendo referencia a la mirada antropológica del cine en los años 20, que grababa en películas el comportamiento de pueblos no europeizados para estudiarlos. Su iniciador fue el francés Robert Flaherty.

este mismo campo dentro del territorio ecuatoriano. A su vez cabe realizar aporte a nuevos y diferentes estudios para la comprensión de los conceptos de cultura, identidad y ancestralidad básicamente, e impulse a yuxtaponer sus significados con otros conocimientos sociales como los de la comunicación y la filosofía específicamente, para intentar vernos de algún modo en términos de Hernán Rodríguez Castello (1993)[4], como "cuna cultural de cosmovisión, sensibilidad e ingenio que fuera pie de inicio para el desarrollo de Latinoamérica toda".

Habría que reconocer que compartimos con algunos pueblos hermanos el despreocupado interés por interrelacionar el concepto cultura con otras disciplinas en estudios sociales. Como consecuencia, por más tiempo del que debiera la poca intención depositada en este tema, ha sido un factor preponderante en las decisiones formativas nacionales, cuyas consecuencias alentaron la apropiación de cierto repertorio distintivo para reivindicar la identidad a través de la imitación vestuario, mal concebido en ocasiones y sin la debida interpretación del significado de una apariencia vernácula que desencaja del entendimiento foráneo, no menos cierto que también sea del entendimiento del nacional.

Evidentemente, por su discusión en varias esferas, el vacío epistémico neo-revolucionario ha hecho réplica en la mirada no muy alentadora de algunos ciudadanos -aunque menos alarmante que hace una década atrás- que prefieren definir como prácticas culturales las apropiaciones y extranjerismos que socavan las esencialidad y propiedad de las representaciones autóctonas (fiestas y celebraciones), la artisticidad de sus diferentes manifestaciones plásticas (la música, la danza, la pintura y la escultura), la oralidad de sus relatos y la sensibilidad hacia la todo lo que vive tan presente en el folklore nacional olvidando acaso que el tipo de ser humano que se forma, forma a su vez un tipo de sociedad.

2. Inconsistencia entre las políticas públicas y el discurso de las Universidades

El trabajo de Bart van der Bijl (2015), vinculado a proyectos de Comunicación y Educación, consultor de ONG y de organismo internacionales

---

4 Hernán Rodríguez Castelo reconocido literato, escritor de muchos y variados textos e historiador de literatura, crítico de arte, ensayista y lingüista ecuatoriano (Quito 1 de junio de 1933 - 20 de febrero de 2017), fue miembro de la Real Academia Española de la Historia y de la Real Academia Española de la Lengua. Entre sus menciones constan el título de Doctor *honoris causa* por la Universidad Central del Ecuador en 2012, la condecoración "Aurelio Espinosa Pólit" por Concejo Metropolitano de Quito en el 2003; el Premio Internacional de Literatura Infantil "Doncel" en 1964 y la Condecoración Española de la orden del Mérito Civil en 1970

de Costa Rica, Holanda y Ecuador, sirve de antecedente para el presente artículo. Analiza la evaluación de carreras universitarias en el Ecuador realizada por el Consejo de Evaluación, Acreditación y Aseguramiento de la Calidad de la Educación Superior, CEAACES y plantea una pregunta interesante ¿desde qué concepción de educación?.

En el proceso evaluativo de estas categorías se dieron uso dos modelos: el general, aplicado en el 2011 con fines de acreditación y el corte genérico en el 2013. La idea era ofertar una educación de calidad definida como la: "búsqueda constante y sistemática de la excelencia, la pertinencia, producción óptima, transmisión del conocimiento y desarrollo del pensamiento mediante la autocrítica, la crítica externa y el mejoramiento permanente" (Art. 93 de la LOES 2010). En el 2013 se evalúa el entorno de aprendizaje de Examen Nacional de Evaluación de Carreras, dirigido a estudiantes del último año.

Por otro lado el Art.28 de la Constitución de la República ecuatoriana que establece que la Educación "se centrará en el ser humano y garantizará su desarrollo holístico en marco del respeto a los derechos, medio ambiente y democracia". Sobre todo a la democracia intercultural, incluyente y diversa, que estimula el sentido crítico y el arte. Este postulado Constitucional (2008) está en concordancia con Plan Nacional del Buen Vivir. (2013-2017), la Propuesta de la Comunidad Educativa para el Plan Decenal de Educación (2016-2025), la Ley Orgánica de Comunicación (2013), la Ley Orgánica de Educación Intercultural (2011), el Proyecto Teleducaciòn (2015) y las funciones de la Educación del Sistema Superior, art. 13, y de la cual, destaca el literal b que precisa la necesidad de "promover la creación, desarrollo, transmisión y difusión de la ciencia, la técnica, la tecnología y la cultura".

Sin embargo a raíz de este examen se mostró inconsistencia entre criterios e indicadores de ambas categorías (la educativa y la comunicativa) en donde fue estimado evaluar el número de participantes y determinados requisitos, sin considerar que la calidad como tal no se puede verificar solo en un cumplimento de requisitos.

Este resultado ameritó de un análisis colateral por parte de las autoras afianzándose en supuestos teóricos y reflexiones filosóficas de autores como:

Gilberto Giménez (2016), relacionado con el estudio de la cultura y de las ideologías desde diversos enfoques como la socio-antropología, la sociología de la cultura, de la identidad, el análisis del discurso, la geo-antropología de la región, así como el concepto de socio-antropología del turismo y un diseño original de la epistemología de las ciencias sociales, como su principal proyecto investigativo.

La participación de Jesús Martín Barbero Barbero (2009), deviene de ideas enmarcadas en el poder de unos influyentes sobre la identidad de otros, que contribuye al enriquecimiento y transformación de los sentidos transdisciplinares.

Además, Paulo Freire (2005), quien a consecuencia del profundo acercamiento que tuvo hacia la educación promulgó la construcción del conocimiento individual, no homogéneo, desde las realidades de los actores. Por una parte, el maestro, guía la construcción del conocimiento del estudiante comenzando con las realidades en las que se desenvuelve, un intento de despertar conciencia acerca de las posibilidades que le rodean brindando la oportunidad de encontrar acciones positivas para la transformación de su propia vida.

Mientras tanto, el estudiante es responsable de construir conocimiento a partir de sus experiencias sensoriales con el entorno próximo y su relación con el profesor, el resultado sería un conocimiento político, crítico, pensante con una postura activa dentro la sociedad, **imbricando categorías del imaginario, que impidan   a la persona funcionar meramente como** receptáculo de información, ya que su finalidad plantearía una opresión del pensamiento que lo llevaría a la memorización mecánica del contenido y al consumo de éste para su reproducción social y no a su desarrollo integral (Bourdieu & Passeron, 1996; Giroux, 2005; Pérez & Gimeno, 2008).

Su práctica ha sido reconocida como una variación de la teología de la liberación una postura específicamente Latinoamericana acreditada a Enrique Dussel. Como fundador de la Filosofía de la liberación, Dussel defiende el "giro descolonizador" o "giro descolonial" una propuesta que se enfoca principalmente en el contexto histórico/sociopolítico Latinoamericano y la participación de sus actores hacia la liberación de América Latina. Sus reflexiones son importantes para esta investigación porque incluyen entre otros temas las ideas cosmogónicas del pensamiento andino alrededor de los Aztecas e Incas, una herencia que compartimos todos los pueblos en América. Desafía directamente la filosofía euroamericana por desacreditar los logros políticos que las culturas egipcia, mesopotámica, china, islámica, azteca, maya e inca, pudieron haber alcanzado.

Boaventura de Sousa Santos se alinea a este pensamiento expresando que:

> Los movimientos del continente latinoamericano, más allá de los contextos, construyen sus luchas basándose en conocimientos ancestrales, populares, espirituales que siempre fueron ajenos al cien-

tismo propio de la teoría crítica eurocéntrica. Por otro lado, sus concepciones ontológicas sobre el ser y la vida son muy distintas del pre-
sentismo y del individualismo occidental. Los seres son comunidades
de seres antes que individuos; en esas comunidades están presentes
y vivos los antepasados así como los animales y la Madre Tierra. Estamos ante cosmovisiones no occidentales que obligan a un trabajo
de traducción intercultural para poder ser entendidas y valoradas
(Souza Santos, 2010, p. 29).

Dussel, profundiza su discurso al estudiar el origen de ciertos términos
y se opone a reconocerlos como iniciáticos de otras culturas que él considera que no fueron su cuna. Más, su crítica hacia diferentes estructuras hegemónicas contemporáneas que son producto de construcciones
históricamente rastreables, las que atan las ideologías y se reproducen
impidiendo el desarrollo evolutivo del pensamiento humano. Su postura
es un impulso a la persistencia de la búsqueda de conocimiento, sin embargo nuestra intención como educadoras no urge al afán de encontrar
culpables entre las páginas de relatos históricos, si no de hallar las huellas que conduzcan a la revalorización, un mirar de vuelta al origen para
encontrar la originalidad y el aprecio por una pugna liberadora que
aúne estas dos últimas propuestas libertarias.

A fin de que a futuro, los ahora educandos pudieran reconocer a decir
de Walter Mignolo que:

> La ciencia (conocimiento y sabiduría) no puede separarse del len-
> guaje; los lenguajes no son sólo fenómenos 'culturales' en los que la
> gente encuentra su 'identidad'; estos son también el lugar donde el
> conocimiento está inscrito. Y si los lenguajes no son cosas que los
> seres humanos tienen, sino algo que estos son, la colonialidad del po-
> der y del saber engendra, pues, la colonialidad del ser. (Schiwy & Mig-
> nolo, 2006, p. 669).

Por último, aunque no menos importante se encuentra Occiel Flores
(1999) al cual le brindamos un espacio más detallado en el siguiente epígrafe. Su relación con la otroredad deja espacios para la reflexión y el
procesamiento comparativo de la información experimentada,

El aporte literario de los autores mencionados hasta ahora, se relacio-
nan a lo largo del documento lo que permite ampliar miradas profundas
al contenido de los resultados para encontrar elementos descriptivos,
característicos, ambiguos, emotivos, fáticos en el discurso articulado
como razón aproximada que respondiera a la pregunta que inicialmente
dio paso a la investigación.

3. Diseño metodológico.

Encontrar la coherencia paradigmática para la metodología cualitativa de esta investigación cuyo enfoque hermenéutico introspectivo vivencial atraviesa el paradigma interpretativo, incluye la revisión teorética de propuestas educativas nacionales y un accionar de técnicas para recoger declaraciones a través de experiencias de vida, epistémicas, societales, individuales y colectivas, que aproximen al discurso manifestado en las aulas del Ecuador, para este caso universitarias. La presencia interdisciplinaria de la trama cientista social sustentó el análisis de los indicadores contenidos en el del discurso articulado.

Los supuestos teóricos encontrados permitieron profundizar en la efectividad de las líneas pedagógicas, investigativas correlacionando la colectividad y las políticas nacionales. Desde esta perspectiva, nos planteamos como educadoras varias interrogantes que dirigieron horizontes en la indagación: Cuáles son las bases en las que se afianza la formación en las universidades ecuatorianas?, ¿Cuáles pueden ser los parámetros de su evaluación? ¿Qué tipo de identidad cultural posee la educación ecuatoriana?,

En el análisis-síntesis de los criterios e indicadores que son de carácter objetivo no se incluyen procesos cualitativos para valorar el pensamiento crítico, el conocimiento conceptual de términos referentes a la revalorización de la identidad, ni la cultura que profesan estudiantes universitarios, ni el sitial que se le da a las Ciencias Sociales en el nuevo milenio. Entonces... cómo entender la descolonización, tan referido en la revolución latinoamericana, desde un contexto de valoración de la otredad? Occiel Flores (1999) en su artículo "Octavio Paz: Otredad, el amor y la poesía", describe la respuesta a esta pregunta. Con el fluido relato de su texto el autor llega a la conclusión que para entender la descolonización habría que tomar conciencia del ser humano, de su individualidad.

Esta orientación refiere a reconocimiento de la existencia del otro y que vive separado. "es la revelación de la pérdida de la unidad del ser del hombre, de la escisión primordial."(ob.cit 1999, p. 1), "La otredad empuja a los seres humanos a buscar al complemento del que fueron separados"(ob.cit 1999, p. 2).

Es decir, la otredad articulada al pensamiento liberador de la colonialidad significa el pueblo pobre, oprimido latinoamericano con respecto a las oligarquías dominadoras. Por ende, surge el latinoamericanismo como expresión de un pensamiento descolonizador para impulsar a la amplitud de los límites disciplinarios y epistemológicos tradicionales asociados a los estudios sobre la cultura y las estructuras de conocimientos en América Latina. A otra lectura de nuestra historia y a reafirmar su valor al desarrollo cultural de la humanidad

De la misma manera, el uso de entrevistas en profundidad a estudiantes, docentes y expertos en comunicación para el desarrollo social, fueron ofrecidas para diferenciar los valores otorgados y su vinculación con la práxis institucional. Los hallazgos fueron analizados con criterios específicos de la categorización del discurso articulado. La triangulación de datos teóricos y empíricos refiere en primera instancia a la presencia de:

- Inconsistencias entre criterios e indicadores de evaluación.

- Énfasis a porcentajes y datos precisos.

- Desconocimiento de procesos.

- Desdibujamiento de significados diversos relativos a la cultura, sus derechos y demandas.

- Desarticulación con la otroredad.

Elementos que superficialmente aparecen como integradores de la relación poco sustancial y poco articulada entre la comunicación y la educación, reflejado en el discurso expresado en las aulas.

4. Analogía en el análisis de los resultados.

Los resultados atraviesan la operacionalización de conceptos y en primera, se enuncia una aproximación inicial a ciertos principios, entre ellos: el diálogo, la participación, la interacción, el empoderamiento ciudadano y el compromiso social, congruentes con la acción educomunicativa propuesta en 2011. Luego dan cuenta de los fenómenos sociales de mayor importancia y pertinencia al estudio para especificar los elementos que componen el discurso en las aulas, los factores que empujan a su uso y a la puntualización de los efectos derivados de la recepción del discurso, que por su jerarquía sirva para orientar al diseño teórica de la construcción funcional y esclarecedora de la descolonización del pensamiento.

La apreciación de Walter Mignolo (2010), permite distinguir este fenómeno como un recurrente suceso de acoplamiento en las sociedades acostumbradas a una visión hegeliana absolutista que al transcurso del tiempo ha distorsionado la mirada conceptual de la cultura, del contexto vital, de las riquezas naturales, así como de su espacio y su tiempo. En términos epistemológicos se antepone a la colonialidad, sin embargo la modernidad necesita de la colonialidad para instalarse, construirse y subsistir. La colonialidad circunda alrededor de la modernidad en pos de permear todos sus espacios. Tal acontecimiento corresponde a lo contrario de la descolonización de pensamiento, por consiguiente a un discurso ajeno a las mencionadas propuestas latinoamericanas configurando en sentido hegemónico, lo que hoy conocemos como pensamiento eurocéntrico retratado en etapas del arte, la política, la historia o la religión de indiscutible presencia en los procesos de enseñanza.

Por tanto, modo de final del proceso analítico, es menester hacer hincapié en que esta investigación por su naturaleza solo ha de considerarse para la aproximación del conocimiento, sino también como una fuente de información para el análisis de las limitaciones y perspectivas de desarrollo educativo, las cuales plantean una discusión de si fomenta o no el pensamiento independiente para argumentar el hecho de autollamarse nación multiétnica y pluricultural. Sabemos lo que debemos ser y esto se recoge en la Constitución de la República (2008), no obstante las contradicciones manifiestas entre la teoría y la práctica en las aulas, especialmente las universitarias en donde se ostenta el derecho a la libertad de cátedra, viabiliza una inevitable confusión a la cual suma una inconsistente conceptualización de definiciones fundamentales que ayudarían al proceso descolonización del pensamiento.

El reconocimiento de los valores inherentes a la ancestralidad de los pueblos testimonio, como llamó Darcy Ribeiro (1992) a países como Paraguay, Perú, México, Guatemala, no forma parte del interés social en Ecuador ni en otras naciones. En este sentido y desde un asiento descolonizador, los medios de comunicación tanto como los procesos de educación escolarizada pueden hacer mucho por devolver a la ciudadanía, y con puntualidad a las comunidades y culturas más directamente vinculadas a estas esencias originarias, una conciencia responsable de autenticidad sobre las matrices culturales, en favor de los procesos de reapropiación cultural de los pueblos históricamente descapitalizados de su pasado histórico-cultural por modelos neoliberales interesados en mantener el presente con propuestas occidentales homogenizantes.

Conclusiones

Al llegar a este punto concluimos que la plataforma sobre la que descansa el discurso académico sudamericano, es emancipador, revalorizante, fortalecedor identitario y consiente de una descolonización cada vez más urgente ante el influjo de la globalización. Sin embargo, a pesar del interés de los grupos descendientes de pueblos testimonio (Ribeiro & Rodríguez Ozán, 1992) se debilita el esfuerzo de quienes habiendo respetado las premisas convenidas internacionalmente por un Buen Vivir, pugnan por la permanencia de su argumento.

La emoción por compartir la esencia cosmogónica andina de la que se hizo eco por algunos años de gobierno en Sudamérica, parece haberse diluido. Los esquemas y paradigmas eurocéntricos socavan las propuestas neoliberales interesadas en el consumo del contenido más que en el pensamiento crítico, pensante y autónomo que en términos de Freire o de Dussel son necesarios para la liberación del pensamiento y el avance de las sociedades Latinoamericanas.

Es urgente reconsiderar la dirección de los estudios sobre la cultura, la identidad, la ancestralidad y otros temas alrededor de estos que brinden definiciones amplias y promuevan reflexiones de conceptos emergentes que pudieran aportar a la comprensión de éstos temas desde otras perspectivas científicas que relacionen el pasado de los pueblos con las manifestaciones actuales. Así representar y no reproducir los saberes ancestrales, revivir no mimetizar la cosmovisión Abya Yala, sentir no solo percibir la esencia cosmogónica de los pueblos ancestrales.

A saber de la existencia de la gran cantidad de textos en la actualidad que defiende el derecho a la presencia de los saberes ancestrales, consideramos importante indicarle al lector que mucha de esta lectura reitera una propuesta de estrecho conocimiento para Latinoamérica que nos mantiene en una visión antropologizada Nuestra intención por incluir las ideas de los autores elegidos para este artículo fue de proponer un visión de fuerte movimiento cambiante para el pensamiento a cuenta de descolonizar los conceptos que tenemos de nosotros mismos, de nuestros hábitos, de nuestras costumbres, abstracciones que desvalorizan nuestras prácticas empujándonos a la pérdida de identidad y a la aculturación de prácticas foráneas sustituyentes de acciones propias de los pueblos originarios.

Los programas nacionales de educomunicación apoyan a subvertir estos actos. A través de los recursos comunicativos, se planifican capítulos que intervienen académicamente en las jóvenes mentes. De manera estratégica se destacan logros, creatividad, valores, propios de nuestra cultura cuyo desconocimiento ha sido implicado en las respuestas sociales, la migración de los ciudadanos y el desinterés por el desarrollo patrio, como fenómenos sociales de mayor relevo.

El carácter instrumental de este proceso investigativo trae como evidencia la inconsistencia que existe entre las políticas públicas y el discurso de las Universidades Nacionales que para evaluar su calidad aplicaron parámetros eurocéntricos, globalizantes y homogéneos haciendo énfasis en porcentajes y datos específicos para encontrar respuestas que debieron ser pensadas en función de las esencialidades de los ecuatorianos y desde la cosmovisión andina. Consideramos acertado el empleo de todas las herramientas cualitativas para la recolección de información puesto que ayudaron a que en el proceso de análisis hubiera mayor visibilidad de los significados obtenidos por los actores sociales y por la teoría revisada.

Asumimos la articulación de las dimensiones educativa y comunicativa como una oportunidad de forja para nuevos y positivos pensamientos que se repliquen en ambientes académicos durante el diálogo de la representación del imaginario del estudiante hacia el profesor o la representación del imaginario del profesor hacia el estudiante. Conscientes de que es un proceso que amerita paciencia para ver el efecto causado por las propuestas educativas nacionales y percibir la transformación de los discursos en las aulas ecuatorianas nos sentimos orgullosas de ver la aceptación de una parte de ciudadanos que independientemente de su postura política, advierten la importancia de reconocer el pasado que fundó el territorio que habitamos.

Asimismo reconocemos que es menester insistir en la inclusión interdisciplinaria de los estudios culturales para sustentar, desde otros puntos de vista (específicamente desde la comunicación), la importancia de su conocimiento. Las limitaciones discursivas tanto como las divergencias en las perspectivas de desarrollo educativo tienen la misma forma, el mismo causal y la misma solución. Lo que resta es apelar a la inventiva del ecuatoriano para encontrar una guía que no solo estimule el pensamiento independiente sino que sirva de referente para los pueblos hermanos de Latinoamérica.

Referentes Bibliográficos.

Definiciones de la cultura — OCW Universidad de Cantabria. (n.d.). Retrieved March 27, 2016, from http://ocw.unican.es/humanidades/introduccion-a-la-antropologia-social-y-cultural/material-de-clase-1/tema-2.-la-cultura/2.3-definiciones-de-la-cultura

Asamblea Nacional. (2018, octubre 20). Ley Orgánica de Educación Superior, LOES. Recuperado de http://aka-cdn.uce.edu.ec/ares/tmp/Elecciones/2%20LOES.pdf

Asamblea Nacional. (2008, October 20). Constitución de la Republica del Ecuador 2008. Retrieved from http://www.ug.edu.ec/talento-humano/documentos/CONSTITUCION%20DE%20LA%20REPUBLICA%20DEL%20ECUADOR.pdf

Boas, F. (1940). Race, Language, and Culture (La raza, el lenguaje y la cultura). The MacMillan company.

Bourdieu, P., Chartier, R., & Darnton, R. (1985). Dialogue à propos de l'histoire culturelle. Actes de la Recherche en Sciences Sociales, 59(1), 86–93. https://doi.org/10.3406/arss.1985.2276

Bourdieu, P., & Passeron, J.-C. (1996). La reproducción. Elementos para una teoría de la enseñanza (2da ed.). México D.F.: Editorial Laia S.A.

Dussel, E. (2018, octubre 8). La transformación de la educación hacia la descolonización de la pedagogía. [MP4]. Recuperado de https://www.youtube.com/watch?v=sWg94cBYDrM

Dussel, E. (2016, October 19). "Sin una descolonización del pensamiento no hay revolución": Enrique Dussel. Retrieved January 30, 2019, from https://lalineadefuego.info/2016/10/19/sin-una-descolonizacion-del-pensamiento-no-hay-revolucion-enrique-dussel/

Flores, O. (1999). Octavio Paz: La otredad, el amor y la poesía. Razón y Palabra Primera Revista Electrónica En América Latina Especializada En Comunicación, 15. Retrieved from http://www.razonypalabra.org.mx/anteriores/n15/oflores15.html

Freire, P. (2005). Pedagogía del oprimido. Siglo Veintiuno Editores.

Galindo, J. (2004). Sistema y Comunicología. Explorando la Complejidad del Mundo Social Contemporáneo. Revista Electrónica Razón y Palabra., 2.

Galindo, J. (n.d.). Comunicología, Comunicación y Cultura. Exploración histórica de dos conceptos centrales en el tránsito del siglo XX al siglo XXI. - Razón y Palabra. Retrieved January 30, 2017, from http://www.razonypalabra.org.mx/N/n66/actual/jgalindo.html

Geertz, C. (1992). Descripción densa: hacia una teoría interpretativa de la cultura. In La interpretación de las culturas (p. 19-40). Barcelona: Gedisa.

Geertz, C. (2003). La Interpretacion de las culturas (duodécima). Barcelona: Gedisa.

Geertz Clifford, & Clifford James. (1998). Genero confusos. La refiguración del pensamiento social. In El surgimiento de la antropología posmoderna (4ta ed.). Barcelona: Gedisa.

Giménez., G. (2012, March 13). "La cultura como identidad y la identidad como cultura." Retrieved February 4, 2018, from https://estudioscultura.wordpress.com/2012/03/13/gilberto-gimenez-la-cultura-como-identidad-y-la-identidad-como-cultura/

Giménez, G. (2016). Estudios sobre la cultura y las identidades sociales. Mexico: ITESO.

Giroux, H. A. (2005). Border Crossings: Cultural Workers and the Politics of Education. (2n edition). New York: Routledge.

https://educacion.gob.ec/wp-content/uploads/downloads/2015/08/PROYECTO_TELEEDUCACION.pdf

http://www.arcotel.gob.ec/wp-content/uploads/downloads/2013/07/ley_organica_comunicacion.pdf

https://educacion.gob.ec/wp-content/uploads/downloads/2017/05/Ley-Organica-Educacion-Intercultural-Codificado.pdf

Ibáñez Etxebarría, A., Vicent Otaño, N., & Asensio Brouard, M. (2012). Aprendizaje informal, patrimonio y dispositivos móviles. Evaluación de una experiencia en educación secundaria. Ibáñez Etxebarría, Alex ; Vicent Otaño, Naiara ; Asensio Brouard, Mikel. Aprendizaje Informal, Patrimonio y Dispositivos Móviles. Evaluación de Una Experiencia En Educación Secundaria. Didáctica de Las Ciencias Experimentales y Sociales; No 26 (2012). Retrieved from http://roderic.uv.es/handle/10550/25677

Jünger Habermas: "Teoría de la Acción Comunicativa".-. (2007, December 18). Retrieved February 1, 2018, from https://aquileana.wordpress.com/2007/12/18/junger-habermas-teoria-de-la-accion-comunicativa/

Marcús, J. (2011). Apuntes sobre el concepto de identidad. Intersticios. Revista sociologica de pensamiento crítico, 5, pág. 107-114.

Martín Barbero, J. (1999). Aventuras de un cartógrafo mestizo en el campo de la comunicación. Revista Latina de Comunicación Social, numero 19. Retrieved from http://www.ull.es/publicaciones/latina/a1999fjl/64jmb.htm

Martín Barbero, J. (2001a). De los medios a las mediaciones. Mexico: Gustavo Gili.

Martín Barbero, J. (2001b). Reconfiguraciones comunicativas de lo público. Anàlisi, 26, 71-88Guadalajara. México.

Martín Barbero, J. (2009, October). "La Universidad vive hoy en el mundo una relación esquizofrénica con la sociedad." La Habana. Retrieved from http://www.cubadebate.cu/opinion/2009/11/02/martin-barbero-habana-conferencia-magistral/

Martínez-Gómez, R., & Agudíez, P. (2012). Comunicación para el Desarrollo Humano: buscando la transformación social. CIC Cuadernos de Información y Comunicación, 17(0), 79–106. https://doi.org/10.5209/rev_CIYC.2012.v17.39259

Oficina Regional de Cultura para America Latina de la Unesco, Perez Casal, C., & Lopez Morales, G. (2000). Cultura y desarrollo. Cuba: Oficina Regional de Cultura para America Latina y el Caribe.

Organización Internacional de trabajo. (2014). Convenio Num. 169 de la OIT sobre Pueblos indígenas y tribales. (Declaración de la ONU) (p. 130). Perú: Naciones Unidas.

Pérez, Á., & Gimeno, J. (2008). Comprender y transformar la enseñanza (12th ed.). España: Ediciones Morata L.S.

Piñero, M. L., & Rivera, M. E. (2013). Investigación cualitativa:Orientaciones Procedimentales. Barquisimeto, Venezuela,: Fondein UPEL.

Ribeiro, D. (1984). La civilización emergente, 17.

Ribeiro, D., & Rodríguez Ozán, M. E. (1992). Las Américas y la civilización: proceso de formación y causas del desarrollo desigual de los pueblos americanos. (M. Pereira Gomes, Ed.) (Vol. 180). Fundación Biblioteca Ayacucho.

Rodríguez, H. (1993). Panorama del Arte (Ministerio de Educación y Cultura: Programa Nacional "Nuevo rumbo Cultural"). Quito-Ecuador: Casa de la Cultura Ecuatoriana.

Schiwy, F., & Mignolo, W. (2006). (Des)colonialidad del ser y del saber: (videos indígenas y los límites coloniales de la izquierda) en Bolivia. (N. Maldonado Torres, Ed.) (Vol. El desprendimiento: Pensamiento crítico y giro des-colonial). Buenos Aires: Ediciones del Signo.

Secretaría Nacional de Planificación y Desarrollo – Senplades. (2013). Plan Nacional del Buen Vivir (primera). Quito, Ecuador. Recuperado de www.buenvivir.gob.ec-, www.planificacion.gob.ec; senplades@senplades.gob.ec

Sousa Santos, B. de. (2010). Refundación del estado en América Latina: perspectivas desde una epistemología del Sur. Plural Ediciones.

van der Bijl, B. (2015, marzo 18). La evaluación de carreras universitarias en el Ecuador ¿Desde qué concepción de educación? Recuperado el 16 de febrero de 2019, de https://universidadsociedadec.wordpress.com/2015/03/18/la-evaluacion-de-carreras-universitarias-en-el-ecuador-desde-que-concepcion-de-educacion/

CONOCIMIENTO CIENTÍFICO EN ACCESO ABIERTO Y LA «MERCANTILIZACIÓN» DE LA ACADEMIA. MÁS ALLÁ DE LA ¿QUIEBRA? DEL NEGOCIO EDITORIAL

D. Luis Arboledas Lérida
Universidad de Sevilla, Estado español

Resumen

El *Open Access* o Acceso Abierto a los resultados de la investigación ha sacudido de arriba abajo el panorama de la Comunicación Científica, acicateado por las posibilidades materiales que Internet y las tecnologías digitales ofrecen, y en consonancia con las exigencias e intereses que cristalizan en y se imponen a través de la política científica. El movimiento o filosofía del *Open Access* aboga por la diseminación libre e irrestricta del conocimiento científicamente sancionado, esto es, por la libertad y gratuidad de acceso a las inscripciones científicas en las que aquel se encuentra fijado, y por la libertad de modificación y reutilización de tales inscripciones.

Varios son los argumentos que se emplean de modo recurrente en defensa de esta nueva forma de concebir la Comunicación Científica. Así, se afirma que la ciencia puede progresar a mayor velocidad si el saber no queda oculto tras los *«paywalls»* de las revistas académicas, evitándose la duplicación de proyectos de investigación con similares objetivos y favoreciéndose, en cambio, la cooperación. También será esta una empresa más transparente y socialmente responsable, en la medida en que el Acceso Abierto permite a cualquier ciudadano conocer de primera mano los resultados de las iniciativas financiadas con dinero público. Más recientemente, y coincidiendo de forma nada casual con la incorporación de disposiciones y mandatos relativos al *Open Access* en las líneas maestras de la política científica, se ha añadido al cuerpo del argumentario una razón, cuanto menos, curiosa: el Acceso Abierto a la ciencia favorece el crecimiento económico, la innovación empresarial y la creación de empleos.

No deja de llamar la atención que del *Open Access* se afirme, por tanto, una cosa y su contraria. Así como los *policy makers* se entusiasman ante la idea de propulsar el desarrollo económico con sólo dar a los empresarios facilidades económicas de uso del saber producido por universidades y Organismos Públicos de Investigación (OPI); así hay autores que señalan, por el contrario, que el Acceso Abierto es un misil en la línea de flotación de la producción capitalista, y señalan a título de ejemplo el hundimiento del negocio editorial basado en el clásico sistema de suscripciones. Por consiguiente, afirman, la generalización de las políticas relativas al *Open Access* no sólo no va a propulsar el beneficio empresarial, sino que, incluso, podría llegar a revertir el proceso de «mercantilización» que acucia a la denominada «ciencia pública».

Lo que este debate dirime, en última instancia, es si puede armonizarse la producción capitalista de valor y plusvalía con la Comunicación Científica libre e irrestricta, cuestión tanto más importante por cuanto que atañe directamente al modo en que las instituciones públicas de investigación se financian con carácter general, esto es, a la estructura de financiación de los Sistemas Nacionales de Ciencia y Tecnología. Este artículo pretende aportar esclarecimiento a la materia, y lo hace enfocando el problema directamente, sin rodeos. Por cuanto que el *Open Access* es resultado de las relaciones de *valor* propias de la organización social capitalista, sólo desde el análisis de tales relaciones sociales de producción es posible poner al fenómeno del Acceso Abierto en sus determinaciones económicas esenciales. La compañía automovilística Tesla, que recientemente ha puesto en abierto el código fuente de dos de los modelos actualmente comercializados, será analizará como caso de estudio.

Palabras claves

Acceso Abierto; Comunicación Científica; Open Access; Tesla; Financiación de la Ciencia; Propiedad Intelectual; Modo de producción capitalista; Marxismo

1. Introducción

La institución científica en su conjunto inició una profunda transformación a partir de la década de los '80 del siglo pasado, un cambio de orden *praxiológico* (Echevarría, 2003); y, más concretamente, de tipo económico. No sólo el progreso tecnológico y el incremento de la productividad social general habían revolucionado de arriba abajo la institución académica; la determinación económica en la que el trabajo científico quedaba puesto también era diferente entonces. La dependencia a las leyes que rigen el mercado y la producción de valor reemplazaba la supeditación a la financiación estatal por parte de los Centros Públicos de Investigación (CPI, en lo sucesivo) que había imperado desde la constitución de los primeros Sistemas Nacionales de Ciencia y Tecnología, allá en los años '30 y '40; y, así, la continuidad del proceso productivo en los *loci* de la «ciencia pública» comenzaba a depender, en grado creciente, de la venta de los productos de su trabajo. Al igual que en el resto de las esferas de la producción capitalista, el valor de cambio (Marx, [1867] 2000, para comprender este concepto) se convierte en mediador generalizado de la actividad científica.

Al margen de y sin aparente conexión con esta revolución en la estructura de financiación de la labor investigadora, una nueva concepción de la Comunicación Científica ha prorrumpido en fechas aún más recientes; concepción que pone el énfasis en la *libertad* y *gratuidad* de acceso al conocimiento fijado en las inscripciones científicas, y, cuanto menos, en la *libertad* de reutilización de tales inscripciones (Piwowar et *al.*, 2018). Hablamos de la filosofía o movimiento del *Open Access*; la cual, tras largo tiempo siendo ignorada en los despachos de la política científica, está ahora recibiendo importantes respaldos por parte de las agencias y programas de financiación más conspicuos, tanto públicos (*Horizon* 2020, la National Science Foundation) como privados (Fundación Bill y Melinda Gates). La presión para poner en abierto los resultados de la investigación resulta especialmente perentoria, en el caso de los CPI, dado que se apoya en un principio frente al que, *prima facie*, no cabe réplica: si el dinero público ha sufragado la investigación, el "público" ha de poder consultar el conocimiento obtenido sin ningún tipo de restricción. Por qué se hace valer este principio *en este momento*, y no hace medio siglo, cuando comenzaron a emerger las primeras grandes editoras de revistas científicas, es algo que este argumento calla en modo deliberado, relevando con ello su carácter oportunista. Mirowski (2018) hace valer otras insuficiencias del argumentario relativo al *Open Access* y la lógica de la «*accountability*» en la que se apoya.

Sea como fuere, a los Centros Públicos de Investigación se les plantea una situación cuanto menos paradojal: de un lado, la política científica los pone en una situación económica tal que sólo la repetida venta de los productos de su trabajo posibilita la renovación constante del proceso productivo, la continuidad de la investigación misma; la «mercantilización» de la ciencia se convierte en una obligación, no en una opción. Del otro, las convocatorias de financiación de proyectos e iniciativas imponen la necesidad de poner a disposición de todo aquel que desee consultarlos, la totalidad de los productos dimanados de esta actividad, ya sea un artículo científico, una base de datos, *softwares*, protocolos o tantos otros (véase, a título de ejemplo, Comisión Europea, 2014). Pues toda inscripción científica susceptible de comunicarse ha de estar en acceso abierto, en especial, cuando es el Estado quien sufraga el trabajo científico, universidades y organismos públicos de investigación pierden suelo bajo sus pies, al ver abortada cualquier tentativa ulterior de valorización de los resultados de investigación. Nadie paga por aquello que puede consultar y utilizar de manera completamente gratuita.

Atrapados en esta contradicción e incapaces de seguir su movimiento dialéctico, algunos autores y activistas creen ver en la generalización de las políticas de *Open Access* un camino expedito para la reversión del nuevo modelo de financiación de la institución científica, la «mercantilización» de la ciencia (caso de Caldera-Serrano, 2018). Fundamentan su feliz vaticinio en que el Acceso Abierto a los resultados de investigación ha hecho saltar por los aires, parcialmente, el negocio editorial de las revistas científicas. O bien alegan que la privatización de la ciencia se sigue, como el 2 sigue al 1 en la sucesión numérica, de la mercantilización de la comunicación científica y el predominio de las grandes empresas editoriales (D'Antonio-Maceiras, 2018); por lo que si el *Open Access* logra quebrar su oligopolio, el trabajo científico dejará de estar sometido a las presiones del mercado.

Ya se ha visto que el impacto de la libre diseminación de los resultados de investigación trasciende, con mucho, la cuestión específica del modelo de negocio editorial de las publicaciones científicas. Sin embargo, estas teorizaciones más o menos quiméricas o fantasiosas tienen su valor, pese a lo restringido de su alcance, en tanto que atañen a la determinación económica esencial del *Open Access*, a saber, la posibilidad o imposibilidad de armonizar la difusión libre e irrestricta de los contenidos de la comunicación científica con la producción de plusvalor y plusvalía. Esta contribución al I Congreso Internacional de Comunicación y Filosofía (Priego de Córdoba, 23 y 24 de noviembre de 2018) se propone abordar y dilucidar tal interrogante desde los parámetros de la Economía Política de la Ciencia, y aportando un caso de estudio digno de atención e interés.

2. Ciencia Abierta... para el capital

Si el Acceso Abierto a los productos de la comunicación científica merece, como proponemos, un examen en términos de *valor*, es precisamente porque esta filosofía o movimiento es resultado necesario de las relaciones de valor que se imponen y dominan en el modo de producción capitalista; y, más concretamente, en el metabolismo social establecido entre la esfera científica y el resto de ámbitos de la producción social. Dicho en forma sucinta: el *Open Access* es producto de unas determinadas *relaciones sociales de producción*, y, como tal, un fenómeno histórico cuya suerte se liga inextricablemente a la de aquellas. Una sociedad cuya reproducción no se rija por la ley del valor, en la que el progreso de la productividad del trabajo no se supedite a la extracción de plusvalía y los productos de la actividad laboral no sean por más tiempo fruto del "trabajo privado" que deviene "social" no directamente, sino mediante un rodeo (ver Marx [1867] 2000; también Rubin, [1923] 1974), no sentirá necesidad de vindicar por más tiempo la liberación de los resultados de investigación.

Los artículos científicos son la principal inscripción que surge de la actividad científica (Latour y Woolgar, 1992), y, por consiguiente, el medio habitual por el que la ciencia entra en relación con otras esferas productivas. No es de extrañar que el Acceso Abierto haya terminado asimilado a esta particular base material del conocimiento científico; que sólo (o preponderantemente) se prescriba que los *papers* han de ser liberados para su consulta y reutilización, dejando al margen el resto de inscripciones. Tanto más justificado se encuentra esto por cuanto que la difusión de los artículos por parte de las revistas académicas se consolidó como el negocio por excelencia organizado en torno a la actividad científica a partir de la segunda mitad del siglo XX (D'Antonio-Maceiras, 2018). Fue en la Comunicación Científica donde la *forma mercantil* de los productos del trabajo académico hizo acto de presencia por primera vez.

La aceptación de los postulados del Acceso Abierto entre académicos, bibliotecarios y activistas va de la mano de su rechazo al negocio editorial (Mirowski, 2018). Internet y las tecnologías digitales habían propiciado una transformación del proceso de trabajo científico del que la comunicación *inter* pares no podía escapar. La Budapest Open Access Initiative (2002) invitaba a las editoriales científicas a adaptarse a este nuevo escenario, buscando modelos de ingresos alternativos a la suscripción convencional. Sin embargo, las campanas parecían doblar incluso por las revistas académicas *qua* artefacto, pues el autoarchivo en repositorios se alzaba como una solución más rápida, eficiente y barata de liberar el conocimiento de las trabas y los tiempos del mundillo editorial.

La incorporación del *Open Access* en los mandatos de la política científica se ha acelerado en la última década, para adquirir ya velocidad de crucero en el último lustro. En su desarrollo histórico, por más breve que éste haya sido, la categoría de «Acceso Abierto» se ha despojado de los ropajes místicos que la envolvían desde su nacimiento, para adoptar su contenido real, la determinación económica que verdaderamente le corresponde. De "unir a la humanidad en una conversación intelectual común" (como se consignaba en la mencionada Budapest Open Access Initiative), el *Open Access* ha pasado a erigirse en "catalizador del crecimiento económico, la innovación y la digitalización de todos los sectores de la economía" (Comisión Europea, 2016). Los «*paywalls*» tras los que las editoriales científicas esconden buena parte de la literatura científica traban el progreso económico y el desarrollo productivo. Si la extensión y generalización de iniciativas que promueven la libre diseminación del conocimiento han de llevarse por delante los capitales invertidos en las revistas científicas[5], estos serán sacrificados en pos de un objetivo más elevado, a saber, la satisfacción de los intereses del capital social total, el capital en su conjunto. De ahí que, por ejemplo, la Comisión Europea elevase recientemente una recomendación a todos los países miembro para lograr que todos los resultados de investigación obtenidos con dinero público sean de libre acceso en 2020. O que la National Science Foundation (NSF) y el National Institute of Health (NIH) estadounidenses, lleven años mandatando Acceso Abierto a toda la literatura científica dimanada de los proyectos por ellos financiados. O que China, Corea del Sur y otras potencias asiáticas estén recabando consejos de sus homólogos occidentales para implementar sus propias políticas de *Open Access* (Else, 2018).

La supervivencia histórica del capital está supeditada a la capacidad que muestre de transformar constantemente la base técnico-material de la producción (Rubin, [1923] 1974), a fin de extraer más plusvalía de menos

---

[5] Las editoriales científicas han mostrado una sorprendente capacidad de adaptación al nuevo escenario, y han comenzado a desarrollar formas alternativas de valorización de sus productos, aun cuando una parte o la totalidad de sus artículos se ofrezcan en Acceso Abierto. Resulta difícil preconizar un hundimiento inminente de estos capitales, a tenor de tal circunstancia.

trabajo (Marx, 2000). Ello lo hace progresivamente dependiente del desarrollo científico y tecnológico, y convierte a la política científica del Estado capitalista en una "política del crecimiento económico" (Hirsch, 1978). Si no se garantizan condiciones favorables a la acumulación del capital, la reproducción social puede quedar en entredicho, como ocurre en épocas de crisis económica (Hirsch, 1978; Mattick, 1975). Si, además, reclama libertad y gratuidad de acceso y reutilización de las inscripciones científicas en las que el conocimiento se fija, ello se debe a su pretensión de descargar sobre el resto de la sociedad una parte creciente de los costes asociados a la adecuación de su estructura productiva a las exigencias de la acumulación. Como dice Mirowski (2018, comillas en el original), "'apertura' y 'transparencia' son expropiación privada *a posteriori*" de la ciencia generada con recursos públicos. Los capitales invertidos en revistas científicas imposibilitaron la libre apropiación del conocimiento por parte de otros capitalistas; la supresión de las barreras técnicas, legales y, sobre todo, económicas propicia que, de nuevo, "la ciencia «ajena» se incorpore al capital lo mismo que el trabajo ajeno" (Marx, [1867] 2000, comillas en el original), esto es, sin que le cueste nada[6].

A este respecto, resulta sintomático el modo en que la OCDE (2015) divide el trabajo entre los diferentes agentes del proceso innovador que lo "abierto" auspicia: desde investigadores individuales hasta compañías editoriales, pasando por gobiernos, agencias de financiación, universidades o bibliotecas; todos movilizan su trabajo y recursos para facilitar la apropiación del conocimiento científico por parte de las empresas, a fin de que se aplique en nuevos productos, servicios y procesos. En sintonía con ello, la Comisión Europea (2016) ha acuñado el concepto de *«Open Innovation»*, con el que refiere a una dinámica de relaciones entre agentes del sistema científico-tecnológico en las que los costes de la transformación tecnológica se reparten entre todos los actores, mas es el capital industrial el que aparece para recoger los beneficios económicos que la investigación produce al final del proceso, sin haber tenido que adelantar y arriesgar su capital en ello (Comisión Europea, 2016, p.12).

---

[6] Como señala Mattick (1977), los capitales individuales crecen y necesariamente han de crecer a costa de otros capitales, aun cuando todos ellos, en forma conjunta, se hermanen en la explotación del trabajo asalariado y se repartan la plusvalía obtenida. No es de extrañar, por tanto, que importantes sectores empresariales reclamen el dejar caer el negocio de las publicaciones científicas si ello les posibilita una reducción de costes.

3. Tesla como caso de estudio. Breves consideraciones sobre el software de los Tesla Model S y Tesla Model X

Hasta aquí, lo "abierto" no ha entrado en conflicto con el beneficio capitalista por cuanto que el capital se ha limitado a apropiarse sin equivalente del conocimiento generado y liberado por otros, en particular, los Centros Públicos de Investigación, gracias al sostén de la financiación pública. Poner esto de relieve no entraña dificultad alguna; de sobra son conocidas las estrategias del capital para descargas sobre el Estado y otros agentes de la producción cuantos costes le sea posible; el *Open Access* es una entre muchas. Encarar la contradicción que el Acceso Abierto podría plantear al modo capitalista de producción, en caso de haberla, requiere de una perspectiva distinta: en lugar de situar a los capitales como *demandantes* de conocimientos en abierto, hay que analizar qué sucede cuando estos ejercen como *productores* de inscripciones científicas diseminadas con derechos de propiedad intelectual no privativos. Uno de estos casos, pequeños en número si bien significativos en grado sumo, es el de la compañía automovilística y de soluciones de energía Tesla.

Tras tiempo haciéndose de rogar, la compañía estadounidense daba a conocer en mayo de 2018 que liberaría los códigos del software de los modelos Model S y Model X protegidos con una licencia no privativa GNU General Public License (GNU-GPL, en lo sucesivo). Puesto que la empresa dirigida por Elon Musk había decidido emplear protocolos de software libre para el desarrollo del Autopilot y los sistemas de infoentretenimiento de sus coches (Moore-Colyer, 2018), protegiendo por este medio su propiedad intelectual, estaba mandatada a poner todo este software en Acceso Abierto. Lo hizo en GitHub, un portal para desarrolladores que, por las mismas fechas, saltaba también a la palestra mediática tras haber sido adquirido por Microsoft por 7.500 millones de dólares. Tanto movimiento empresarial en torno a lo "abierto" no deja, desde luego, de llamar la atención.

No era la primera vez que Tesla se desmarcaba del resto de competidores con un movimiento semejante. En 2014, la controvertida empresa anunciaba que ponía a libre disposición de quien deseara usarlas, las 200 patentes que tenía concedidas (Musk, 2014). Sus argumentos torales eran dos: 1) las patentes no protegen contra las violaciones de la propiedad intelectual por compañías rivales; 2) las patentes frenan, más que impelen, la innovación y el progreso del coche eléctrico. Por consiguiente, el fabricante de automóviles se comprometía a no denunciar a quien "en buena fe, haga uso de nuestra tecnología" (Musk, 2014). *Mutatis mutandi*, similares argumentos podrían haber sido empleados en el caso del software. Cualquiera, con o sin cuenta en GitHub, puede descargar el código que rige para dos de los tres modelos actualmente comercializados por Tesla, con derecho a leerlo, modificarlo y reutilizarlo sin ninguna restricción.

4. Las potencialidades económicas de lo abierto

Cuando el fabricante estadounidense dio a conocer su propósito de liberar las más de doscientas patentes que tenía concedidas, algunos medios de comunicación apuntaron con perspicacia la lógica económica que subyacía a este movimiento estratégico. Así, la lectura que se hacía desde el periódico español ABC (2014) era que una eventual expansión del coche eléctrico auspiciada por la adopción masiva de las patentes de Tesla, permitiría que ésta ampliase su negocio, no ya fabricando coches, sino proveyendo al resto de competidores de *sus* baterías de litio y brindando *sus* sistemas de recarga —una flota mayor de vehículos usando estos súper-cargadores permitiría una más rápida amortización de los mismos; objetivo harto deseable dada la escasa penetración de Tesla en mercados como el europeo. El fabricante automovilístico californiano podría adquirir así una posición de predominio en el mercado del turismo eléctrico generalista, aunando la producción de coches con la producción de componentes y sistemas para vehículos de otras marcas.

A nadie escapa que si el capitalista (véase por caso, el señor Musk) decidiese facilitar el uso libre e irrestricto de todo aquello que produjese, si el valor de uso de sus productos se pudiese enajenar gratis, a cambio de nada, pronto dejaría de ser capitalista. El beneficio económico se obtiene en la producción mercantil, no en su circulación (Arrizabalo, 2018, para una exposición asequible pero completa de esta cuestión), mas la plusvalía extraída *ha de valorizarse en el mercado, cambiarse por dinero*, si se quiere retomar el ciclo productivo. Tesla no produce coches eléctricos para salvar el planeta, ni para el mero regocijo de su histriónico CEO. Los crea para obtener un beneficio económico de la explotación de la fuerza de trabajo asalariada en sus fábricas y departamentos. Si sus Model S o Model X estuviesen en "acceso abierto" y cualquiera los pudiese usar de forma gratuita, pronto buscarían Musk y el resto de los inversores de la compañía un nuevo empleo productivo para su dinero.

La clave de esta osada estrategia empresarial reside en que Tesla *produce y vende coches, no así inscripciones científicas*. Si puede conceder a otros competidores el uso y disfrute de estas últimas, es precisamente porque la valorización de su capital no depende de que tales inscripciones hallen comprador en el mercado. Más generalmente, la obtención de licencias privativas de propiedad intelectual cae dentro de los denominados *faux frais* [gastos falsos, gastos improductivos] de la producción, a los que ya se refiriese Marx ([1867] 2000). Las patentes[7] son resultado de los esfuerzos que hace el capital para generar beneficio aun cuando no puede, cuando, simplemente, circula en su *forma mercantil*. Incluso a expensas de ver violentada su propiedad intelectual, Tesla renuncia sin embargo a asumir esos *faux frais*. Al cambio, podría ganar con ello tanto una reducción de costes como una penetración en nichos de negocio que tendría vedados de otro modo. El negocio parece redondo. Pero, en realidad, resta todavía por dilucidar cómo es posible que Tesla logre obtener beneficio con unas tecnologías que *no puede* valorizar, que ha puesto a disposición de todo el mundo para que se utilicen sin equivalente alguno.

Más arriba ya se consignó que los diversos capitales, acicateados por la competencia entre sí, necesitan de incorporar el conocimiento científico, técnico y tecnológico para obtener plusvalía en forma constante y siempre creciente. En consecuencia, la ciencia se incorpora al capital en un doble sentido. Desde un punto de vista general, teórico, aquélla se convierte en encarnación, no ya del progreso social ni de la creciente productividad del trabajo, sino de la fuerza productiva del capital (Marx, [1867] 2000). Conforme a una consideración más sobre terreno, las inscripciones científicas se convierten en un elemento de la producción más a sumar al proceso de trabajo, cuya naturaleza específica y forma de fijación material (máquina, software, protocolo, o, incluso, un simple artículo) vendrán dados en virtud de la propia naturaleza del proceso productivo en el cual son movilizadas. Sin embargo, el conocimiento *no puede incorporarse al proceso de trabajo sin coste alguno*, aun cuando se encuentre a libre disposición de los capitales (como ocurre con la tecnología de Tesla); la reutilización de una inscripción científica en un proceso de trabajo distinto de aquel en el que surgió, no puede hacerse sino a expensas de incurrir en costes adicionales, costes que van más allá del pago por acceso.

Callon (1994) identificó hasta cuatro epígrafes de gasto (él los denominaba «inversiones», un término que no nos parece el más adecuado)

---

[7] Para Dickson (1988), las patentes son "conocimiento en su forma mercantil pura". Sin que ello deje de ser cierto, una consideración más amplia nos permitiría ver en ellas la quintaesencia de las relaciones de producción capitalista: apropiación privada del conocimiento (del trabajo) obtenido en un proceso productivo cada vez más socializado. Las patentes y los derechos de propiedad intelectual constatan lo que es, en sí, una obviedad, a saber, que el capitalista *es propietario simultáneamente del proceso de trabajo y del producto del mismo*.

diferentes que se presentaban allí donde pretendíase dar un *uso productivo* a cualquier inscripción científica. Estos serían:

- **Coste de acceso y reproducción** a la inscripción científica[8]. Por «reproducción» de la inscripción científica ha de entenderse el cambio de soporte material en el que el conocimiento queda objetivado (verbigracia, simulando mediante *software* una tecnología de la que se dispone un ejemplar físico, o viceversa). Estos gastos son insignificantes, según Callon, en relación con el resto, pero no por ello dejan de estar presentes.

- **Coste de los bienes complementarios**. Instrumentos, maquinaria, materias primas o capacitaciones profesionales; conocimientos adicionales, en suma, que se necesitan para dotar de sentido una determinada inscripción.

- **Coste de mantenimiento de los bienes complementarios**, en particular, gasto en los medios de vida (salarios) de técnicos e investigadores contratados.

- **Coste de la «reconfiguración productiva» de la inscripción científica**. Cualquier inscripción necesita adaptarse a los fines del nuevo proceso productivo al que se incorpora para resultar verdaderamente útil; y ello comporta su completa transformación.

Bien como coste, bien como inversión, lo que Callon (1994) pone en relieve es que la movilización de un determinado conocimiento científico al proceso productivo requiere, además de la inscripción en la que se encuentra fijado, toda una serie de factores de producción adicionales que se han de incorporar junto con aquella, y que, por consiguiente, alguien ha de producir. De ahí deduce él que el saber científicamente sancionado no puede ser un «bien público», a diferencia de lo que sostenía la ortodoxia neoclásica de la época[9]. Nosotros, por nuestra parte, nos apoyamos en este principio para sostener que aun la implementa-

---

[8] Callon sólo incluye en este epígrafe los costes de reproducción, no así los de acceso. En su hipótesis de trabajo, la ciencia es un «bien público», *ergo* el acceso a las inscripciones es libre y gratuito. No obstante, si se hace a un lado tal punto de partida, es necesario incluir tales costes en este apartado, en tanto que no se puede reproducir en una base material diferente una inscripción que no se ha podido consultar.

[9] Aunque no sea cuestión que se haya de abordar aquí, sí que merece la pena mencionar, al pasar, que tanto Callon como aquellos con los que polemizaba, cometían el error de buscar en las propiedades materiales del conocimiento el fundamento a las relaciones de valor (*relaciones sociales de producción*) articuladas al interior de la esfera de la producción científica.

ción más intensiva y extensiva del *Open Access* no puede, en última instancia, reducir a 0 el coste de la transformación de la base técnico-material de los diferentes capitales en concurrencia. Desde esta perspectiva, la distinción habitual que se hace entre lo que es "libre" y lo que es "gratuito", cobra un nuevo significado. Ya era sabido que se requiere de tiempo de trabajo para producir el conocimiento científico puesto en *Acceso Abierto*. Ahora, se constata también que no sin esfuerzo[10] (tiempo de trabajo socialmente necesario) puede adquirir éste utilidad en un proceso productivo diferente.

Precisamente porque esos gastos en los que el capital incurre para incorporar nuevo conocimiento a su proceso de trabajo existen y son inevitables, Tesla se halla en condiciones de *hacer negocio con el Acceso Abierto*, por decirlo de un modo grueso. Bajo la égida de las relaciones sociales de producción capitalistas, el hecho de que el conocimiento científico no pueda incorporarse sino entregando un equivalente, se manifiesta como ineluctable necesidad de reducir al mínimo el coste en el que los capitales incurren a tal efecto. Si cada empresa que usara las tecnologías de Tesla, tuviese que adelantar el capital para adquirir y explotar por sí misma todos los factores productivos enumerados más arriba, a fin de lograr una apropiación efectiva de aquel conocimiento, la ruina estaría garantizada para la mayoría. En cambio, Tesla ya posee y moviliza todos esos recursos productivos, destinados sólo a la producción de *sus* coches. Y no todos pueden ponerse en abierto, a decir verdad, por más que avance la tecnificación de la actividad productiva y pueda codificarse el conocimiento humano (Nieto, 2018)[11]. La propia compañía californiana se encuentra en las mejores condiciones para proveer a otras de servicios y productos que faciliten la adopción de sus patentes y su código en los más diversos procesos productivos; al cambio, aquellas otras compañías habrán de adelantar un capital significativamente menor. Mediante la provisión de todo aquello que el resto de

---

10 Guerrero (2018) y Astarita (2018) combaten las falencias sobre la que se sostiene la teoría subjetivista del valor aduciendo que el valor de cambio de cualquier producto no puede deberse a la *utilidad* que el comprador le otorga (real o imaginada) o a su grado de *escasez*, puesto que la escasez "es una relación social" (Astarita, 2018); o, bien, que algo es escaso en tanto que está "mediado por el trabajo" (Guerrero, 2018). Más concretamente, la base material del valor, son los esfuerzos sistemáticos que se hacen en pos de un determinado fin, de la obtención y reproducción de cualquier cosa útil. Lo que nada cuesta obtener, nada puede valer.

11 El citado Nieto (2018) olvida que la "maquinaria viva de la producción" (Marx, *Teorías*), la fuerza de trabajo o capacidad laboral, adquiere en el curso del proceso productivo una formación, un grado de instrucción y pericia, dados en primer término por la propia experiencia, que no pueden separarse de la corporeidad humana, tal y como la mercancía que el obrero vende al capitalista no puede desgajarse de sí mismo, de su propio ser (Marx, [1867] 2000).

fabricantes de automóviles eléctricos no podrían adquirir por sí mismos, la empresa de Elon Musk puede ampliar su cuota de mercado y extraer una plusvalía adicional sin que el capital invertido por ella tenga que crecer en la misma proporción, aumentando, con ello, la tasa y la masa de beneficio (Marx, [1867] 2000, para comprender bien la diferencia entre *plusvalía* y *ganancia*). Pero abrirse hueco como proveedor de soluciones tecnológicas para otros fabricantes pasa por ofrecer incentivos para la utilización de las inscripciones científicas propias, verbigracia, brindándolas en *Acceso Abierto*. He aquí la racionalidad económica subyacente al *Open Access* desde el lado de la oferta empresarial.

5. *Open Access* y «mercantilización» de la ciencia. Implicaciones para los CPI

Así las cosas, hemos arribado a la conclusión de que la libre diseminación del conocimiento científico (la Comunicación Científica, en sentido lato) por parte de las empresas, no sólo no repercute negativamente en sus beneficios, sino que, más bien al contrario, podría coadyuvar a su incremento. Esta relación no conflictiva entre ambas dimensiones responde a que: i) el conocimiento científico no es el producto resultante del proceso de trabajo (aun cuando rezume por todos sus poros[12]), sino tan sólo una externalidad del mismo; ii) por consiguiente, no todo el saber científico es o puede ser deslindado (objetivado) del proceso productivo mismo, comenzando por aquel que se hipostasia en la misma fuerza laboral, en el «obrero colectivo» (Marx, [1867] 2000). Se resuelve así el interrogante que servía de punto de partida a este trabajo: ¿existe posibilidad de armonizar la diseminación de las inscripciones científicas en Acceso Abierto con la producción de valor y plusvalía, con la producción capitalista? Desde luego que es posible. Incluso cuando son los mismos capitales privados los que proveen de ese conocimiento en abierto, ello no tiene por qué entrar en conflicto con la obtención de beneficios, siempre que se cumplan las dos condiciones antemencionadas. No obstante, la ley se cancela allí donde estos requisitos no se verifican. Y ello nos remite, inmediata e irremisiblemente, al ámbito de la actividad académica.

El trabajo de los Centros Públicos de Investigación (CPI) tiene por finalidad la obtención de *nuevas* inscripciones científicas. Eso es lo que diferencia la esfera de la producción científica de todas las demás. El *consumo productivo* de material, instrumento y trabajo vivo, los elementos productivos (Marx, [1867] 2000) en los que el conocimiento previo

---

[12] No por menos, Marx ([1867] 2000) consideraba al saber científico como pináculo del desarrollo de las fuerzas productivas del trabajo.

puede presentarse incorporado o junto a estos, se orienta hacia la obtención de una *nueva inscripción científica*, nuevos valores de uso que son, dada su misma cualidad material, conocimiento, saberes que sirven a los humanos para extender y profundizar su dominación intelectual y material de la naturaleza[13] (entendida como naturaleza social, históricamente producida. Véase, Marx, [1867] 2000).

Esta circunstancia niega los dos supuestos materiales sobre los que se erigía la relación armoniosa entre producción capitalista y Acceso Abierto. Las inscripciones científicas no son aquí una externalidad que emana de forma más o menos incontrolable del proceso de trabajo, sino el fin hacia el que éste se orienta. Asimismo, o, más bien, debido a ello, el grado de codificación que se exige del conocimiento es mucho mayor, pues, en tanto que producto del trabajo, en él se han de *objetivar*, como resultado neutro, los insumos que productivamente han sido consumidos. En las fábricas de conocimiento que son universidades y OPI, la generalización y extensión de las políticas sobre *Open Access* viene a retirar la base bajo sus pies, el suelo donde había de encontrar arraigo el nuevo paradigma de financiación de la «ciencia pública».

El Acceso Abierto no tendría mayor impacto en la estructura de la financiación de la ciencia de no ser porque la política científica ha empujado a los Centros Públicos de Investigación a convertirse en unidades formalmente independientes respecto del Estado y la contribución estatal a sus arcas (proceso que va más allá de la mera retracción del gasto público en I+D). Ahora, los CPI están en la obligación de comercializar la *ciencia* que producen; ésta es su mercancía. Y así como decíamos que Elon Musk no podía regalar sus Tesla, ponerlos en "libre acceso", sin verse muy pronto privado de su capital, así estas unidades de producción no pueden brindar gratis su producto, so pena de ver dinamitada esa vía de ingresos. Pero es precisamente lo que le exigen, en modo creciente, las agencias de financiación (tanto públicas como privadas) y, más generalmente, la política científica en su conjunto. La continuidad del proceso productivo al interior de estos *loci* del conocimiento queda, por tanto, en entredicho, en la medida en que encuentran dificultades adicionales —más allá de las que el mismo mercado impone, que no son pocas— para vender la mercancía y volver a adquirir los medios de producción empleados (pagar salarios, comprar instrumental o maquinaria, etcétera).

---

[13] El conocimiento de las leyes que rigen la naturaleza adquiere condición de fuerza productiva en tanto que permite poner aquella al servicio de la reproducción social. Por consiguiente, esta búsqueda de la ampliación de la dominación material sobre la naturaleza exterior del hombre, es y debe de ser el *perpetuum mobile* de la investigación y la ciencia.

La contradicción está servida y resulta harto evidente: la política científica pública espolea que el valor de cambio se convierta en "mediador generalizado de la producción" (Marx, [1971] 2005) también en el caso de los centros de investigación; pero, al mismo tiempo, obstruye parcialmente esta posibilidad al obligar a poner en abierto los resultados del trabajo científico financiado con dinero público. Cegada la vía de intercambiar con otros productores privados, el Estado comienza a erigirse en el único *comprador*, en el único demandante con poder de compra suficiente, para la adquisición de los resultados de investigación. El *Open Access* comporta, en última instancia, una *mayor dependencia* por parte de los CPI de la financiación pública. Exactamente lo opuesto de lo que pretendía el nuevo modelo de financiación de la ciencia que a partir de la década de los '80 comenzó a implantarse a nivel global.

Como se dijo en §1, hay autores que están tentados a colegir de ello que la reversión de los cambios introducidos en la estructura de financiación de la ciencia es material e históricamente posible *gracias* al Acceso Abierto, que se erige en medio para lograr tan deseable objetivo. Sin embargo, toda su quimérica construcción se desmorona cuando se para mientes en un pequeño detalle: la extensión del *Open Access* a tenor de las políticas científicas públicas y las convocatorias de financiación a proyectos precipita la transformación unilateral del trabajo científico, no ya con vistas al valor de cambio sin más (*producción mercantil*), sino a la satisfacción de las exigencias impuestas por el Estado en tanto que *demandante con capacidad adquisitiva, poder de compra autónomo* (Luxemburgo, 1978). Como en cualquier otro acto de la circulación mercantil simple, comprador (véase, el Estado) y vendedor (esto es, los CPI) se enfrentan como propietarios de mercancías que proceden a intercambiar. El primero pretende enajenar el valor de uso del producto que el segundo le ofrece; la naturaleza material de este último ha de estar, pues, en consonancia con las necesidades de aquel. Cuando su capacidad efectiva de compra le permite participar en muchos intercambios, atraer a sí un gran volumen de vendedores, el comprador se encuentra entonces en condiciones de determinar los requisitos indispensables que el producto ha de cumplir si los productores desean recibir dinero a cambio. Son las bases y pliegos de condiciones de las convocatorias de ayudas a proyectos de investigación las que recogen las exigencias que el Estado, como comprador, impone a los Centros Públicos de Investigación (vendedores-productores) que desean concurrir y ganar estas.

Las presiones económicas que acucian a los CPI no desaparecen, sino que transmutan y se trasladan, desde la venta sin más de los resultados del trabajo científico a cualquier comprador, a la captación de recursos para proyectos de investigación en las convocatorias competitivas. En el modo de producción capitalista, aseveraba Marx ([1867] 2000), no sólo se producen mercancías, sino las *relaciones sociales de producción* que a éstas subyacen. Al final del proceso de intercambio entre CPI y los agentes de financiación públicos descrito, los primeros vuelven a aparecer como productores-vendedores, y los segundos, en cambio, de nuevo como compradores. El Acceso Abierto a la Comunicación Científica, por cuanto que obstruye cualquier posibilidad ulterior de valorización de los resultados de investigación, cataliza este desarrollo unilateral del trabajo científico. El *Estado* es el *mercado* para la ciencia, y a su voluntad se subsumen los Centros Públicos de Investigación.

6. En conclusión

Las disquisiciones en torno al fenómeno del *Open Access* se han mantenido hasta la fecha en un terreno eminentemente bibliográfico, enfoque predilecto para cuestiones de Comunicación Científica. De ahí que, cuando se alude a su posible impacto económico, sólo alcance a hablarse de revistas científicas y modelos de negocio editorial. A expensas de ver y testimoniar si, y cómo, el Acceso Abierto repercute en las modalidades tradicionales de venta de las publicaciones académicas, basadas en suscripciones, poco más de importancia cabe decir ya al respecto. Además, la clave para comprender este fenómeno en sus determinaciones económicas esenciales no se encuentra aquí. En tanto que el *Open Access* es resultado necesario de las relaciones de valor capitalistas, resulta indispensable, por lo tanto, enfocar el análisis desde esta perspectiva.

El capital demanda la libre diseminación de los resultados de investigación para poder incorporar el conocimiento sin equivalente alguno, de forma completamente gratuita. Descarga sobre otros (el Estado, en primer término) el coste de la transformación de su base técnico-material, progresivamente más dependiente del progreso científico. Los Centros Públicos de Investigación quedan mandatados para proveer de esas inscripciones científicas de uso libre, irrestricto y gratuito. Pero ello comporta que entregan sin equivalente los productos de su trabajo. Si no logran valorizar en el mercado los resultados de su investigación, no podrán readquirir los factores productivos necesarios para dar continuidad al proceso productivo. El Acceso Abierto y el nuevo paradigma de financiación de la ciencia se repelen mutuamente, y la contradicción que se plantea amenaza con obstruir el progreso científico, técnico y tecnológico del que tan dependiente es el capital.

Junto con otros factores, el Acceso Abierto viene a poner a los CPI en una dependencia mayor, y no menor, de la financiación pública de la investigación. Mas ello no redunda en una aminoración de las presiones económicas que acucian a los *loci* de la «ciencia pública». Más bien, el *Estado* es el *mercado* para los productos del trabajo científico, y los CPI han de subsumirse a las necesidades y exigencias que los estados hagan valer, en tanto que *demandantes*, que *poder de compra autónomo*, a través de sus agencias y programas de financiación de proyectos.

7. Bibliografía

ABC (2014). Tesla libera sus 200 patentes para facilitar la fabricación de los coches eléctricos. Recuperado de: https://www.abc.es/tecnologia/informatica-hardware/20140613/abci-tesla-libera-patentes-ayudar-201406131638.html

Arrizabalo, Xabier (2018). Explotación (y creciente): base material del capitalismo, piedra angular del análisis marxista. En Guerrero, Diego y Nieto, Maxi (eds.), Qué enseña la economía marxista. 200 años de Marx. Barcelona: El Viejo Topo.

Astarita, Rolando (2018). Crítica, desde un enfoque marxista, a la teoría austriaca del valor. En Guerrero, Diego y Nieto, Maxi (eds.), Qué enseña la economía marxista. 200 años de Marx. Barcelona: El Viejo Topo.

Caldera-Serrano, Jorge (2018). La ciencia que financiamos y repagamos. El Salto Diario. Disponible en: https://www.elsaltodiario.com/saltamos-extremadura/la-ciencia-que-financiamos-repagamos

Callon, Michel (1994). Is science a public good? Fifth Mullins Lecture, Virginia Polytechnic Institute. Science, Technology & Human Values, 19 (4), pp. 395-424.

Comisión Europea (2014). Horizon 2020, en breve. El Programa Marco de la Investigación y la Innovación en la Unión Europea. Luxemburgo: Publications Office of the European Union.

Comisión Europea (2016). Open Innovation, Open Science, Open to the World – a vision for Europe. Luxemburgo: Publications Office of the European Union.

Comisión Europea (2018). Horizon 2020 Programme. AGA – Annotated Model Grant Agreement, versión 5.0. Recuperado de http://ec.europa.eu/research/participants/data/ref/h2020/grants_manual/amga/h2020-amga_en.pdf

D'Antonio-Maceiras, Sergio. El círculo vicioso de las revistas científicas y la progresiva irrelevancia de la ciencia pública. Política y Sociedad, 55 (2), pp. 467-490. DOI: http://dx.doi.org/10.5209/POSO.57222

Dickson, David (1988). The new politics of science. Chicago: University of Chicago Press.

Echevarría, Javier (2003). La revolución tecnocientífica. Madrid: Fondo de Cultura Económica.

Else, Holly (2018). Europe's open-access drive escalates as university stand-offs spread. Nature. Recuperado de: https://www.nature.com/articles/d41586-018-05191-0

Guerrero, Diego (2018). La teoría laboral del valor y la crítica de la teoría neoclásica. En Guerrero, Diego y Nieto, Maxi (eds.), Qué enseña la economía marxista. 200 años de Marx. Barcelona: El Viejo Topo.

Hirsch, Joachim (1978). The state apparatus and social reproduction: Elements of a theory of the bourgeois State, en Holloway, John & Piccioto, Sol (Eds.), State and Capital. A marxist debate. Londres: Edward Arnold Publishers.

Latour, Bruno y Woolgar, Steve (1990). La vida en el laboratorio. Madrid: Alianza Editorial.

Luxemburgo, Rosa (1978). La acumulación del capital. Ciudad de México: Grijalbo.

Marx, Karl (2000/1867). El Capital. Crítica de la Economía Política. Barcelona: Akal.

Marx, Karl (2005/1971). Elementos fundamentales para la crítica de la Economía Política: (Borrador) 1857-1858. México: Siglo XXI editores.

Mattick, Paul (1975). Marx y Keynes. Los límites de la economía mixta. Buenos Aires: Razón y Revolución.

Mirowski, Philip (2018). The future(s) of Open Science. Social Studies of Science, 48 (2). DOI: https://doi.org/10.1177/0306312718772086

Moore-Colyer, Roland. Tesla open sources some of its Autopilot source code. The Inquirer. Recuperado de: https://www.theinquirer.net/inquirer/news/3032649/tesla-open-sources-some-of-its-autopilot-source-code

Musk, Elon (2014). All our patent are belong to you. Recuperado de: https://www.tesla.com/blog/all-our-patent-are-belong-you

Nieto, Maxi (2018). La eficiencia dinámica en una economía planificada. En Guerrero, Diego y Nieto, Maxi (eds.), Qué enseña la economía marxista. 200 años de Marx. Barcelona: El Viejo Topo.

Organización para la Cooperación y el Desarrollo Económicos (2015). Making Open Science a reality, OECD Science, Technology and Industry Policy Papers, 25. Paris: OECD Publishing. DOI: https://doi.org/10.1787/5jrs2f963zs1-en.

Piwowar, Heather et *al.* (2018). The state of OA: a large-scale analysis of the prevalence and impact of Open Access articles. PeerJ, 6:e4375. DOI: https://doi.org/10.7717/peerj.4375

Rubin, Isaak Illich (1975/1923). Ensayos marxistas sobre la teoría del valor. Buenos Aires: Ediciones Pasado y Presente.

EL ESTADO CAPITALISTA COMO ENTE RESTAURADOR Y COMUNICACIONAL EN LAS CONCEPCIONES DE HEGEL

Mgtr. Tomás Rodríguez Caguana
Universidad de Guayaquil, Ecuador

Mgtr. Guadalupe Vernimmen Aguirre
Universidad de Guayaquil, Ecuador

Resumen

Este trabajo de investigación aborda el problema del Estado como ente restaurador y regulador en la Filosofía de Hegel. La Filosofía Política reconoce la dificultad de prescribir "la noción ideal de un Estado", abordando categorías como "Ciudadano", "Sociedad", "Cultura", "Ley", "Derechos", entre otras. Desde las ciudades-estado griegas (teniendo la Guerra del Peloponeso su punto cardinal), hasta Habermas y Badiou, la Filosofía Política genera premisas para interpretar al Estado y a la sociedad, dependiendo de los momentos históricos-económicos contemporáneos. La comunicación, a inicios del siglo XIX, en plena expansión del Capitalismo como modo de producción global, colaboró con el ordenamiento, regulación, distribución y normalización de los procesos económicos, industriales y sociales.

El problema que aborda este trabajo es ¿cómo se constituyen los fundamentos filosóficos del Estado en la concepción hegeliana y su relación con las concepciones comunicacionales de distribución y regulación? El objetivo general de esta ponencia busca identificar las categorías filosóficas-hegelianas y las comunicacionales-industriales que contribuyeron a la constitución del Estado capitalista como eje fundamental de la Revolución Industrial. La comunicación emerge como un sistema social que acompaña a la humanidad y a occidente en los procesos de lo que Hegel identifica como la modernidad, asir de la subjetividad. En el contexto pre-capitalista, de la ilustración, la revolución industrial, el nacimiento de las ciencias modernas, en el análisis filosófico hegeliano, se entiende que la comunicación es un eje para comprender unas condiciones propias de la regulación y control hegemónico de la economía y sociedad contemporánea, lo condujo a la construcción del estado-nación y el proyecto de la modernidad. Emerge lineal, unidireccional, en serie y repetitiva. Lo que se encuentre por fuera de ese orden mandatorio, es deslegitimado. La comunicación cumple una función regulatoria y normalizadora en tanto estandariza y clasifica unos valores occidentales, considerándolos válidos en contraste con otros, subordinados y de escaso o nulo valor. Los valores de la modernidad como proyecto político, social y económico estandariza a las sociedades "modernas", y con ello todas las ideologías que sustentan el status quo y la legitimación del orden social. Desde la comunicación, se establecen órdenes dicotómicos entre modernos e incivilizados. Este proceso tiene un tipo de investigación descriptivo, un diseño no experimental-transeccional, una metodología hermenéutica, y desarrolla técnicas cualitativas. La bibliografía se basa en los textos clásicos de Hegel: *Filosofía de la Historia; Filosofía Real; Fenomenología del Espíritu.* Su contraposición en Schopenhauer: *El mundo como voluntad y representación.* El análisis histórico de Mattelart en: *Historias de las Teorías de la Comunicación.* Finalizando con los debates actuales de Badiou y Žižek en *Filosofía y actualidad. El debate.*

Palabras claves

Comunicación, Filosofía, Política, Modernidad, Sociedad, Control

Introducción

El desarrollo de las fuerzas pre-capitalistas tuvo en distintas escuelas filosóficas un colaborador fundamental. Desde Francis Bacon, con sus preceptos de materialismo mecanicista, Thomas Hobes en *el Leviatan* que manifestaba la necesidad de un mínimo de organización social, las distintas perspectivas iban ya configurando el nuevo modo de producción que guia al mundo en las siguientes centurias hasta la actiualidad.

La propia filosofía política con Nicolás Maquiavelo en Italia construía contenidos que mostraban la necesidad de que las nuevas élites comerciales, mercantilistas iban a requerir, para la transición de dejar a un lado la cosmovisión feudal, nuevos esquemas de control social, liderazgo y articulación de relaciones que reemplazaría la total verticalidad con la que se manejaba la aristocracia europea.

Incluso en escuelas en que supuestamente el objeto de estudio se concentraba en las formas en que se construía el conocimiento (racionalismo, empirismo) se analizan ya los esquemas fundacionales del posterior capitalismo. La duda cartesiana, la nueva interpretación sobre Dios en Spinoza, las formas de conocimiento humano en John Locke, la interpretación de las dinámicas científicas en David Hume, demuestran que esas dos teorías filosóficas que dominaron no solo el escenario franco-anglosajón sino a toda Europa en los siglos XVII y XVIII no estuvieron ajenas a la interpretación de los nuevos esquemas económicos, sociales, culturales, que ocurrían en el viejo continente.

En la *Ilustración francesa* el sujeto analizado, ya es un ser plenamente capitalista puesto que el desarrollo de las fuerzas productivas y su avance progresivo en Inglaterra y Países Bajos, mostraban que la transición era inevitable. El *sujeto de la Ilustración* es universal, cosmopolita, con derecho a tener derechos, cuestionador de las formas eclesiales, monárquicas y de sus mandantes. Completamente liberal en su economía, su interpretación de las ciencias y del mundo. Es, sin duda, la Ilustración el marco teórico de la Revolución francesa. Las escuelas posteriores a la revolución francesa fueron totalmente tributadoras o reinterpretativas de ese hecho trascendental acontecido en 1789. Kant, desde el *Idealismo trascendental* ya menciona completamente al mundo capitalista cuando establece el *categórico imperativo*, como también las relaciones fenoménicas y nouménicas como espacios de conocimiento y posibilidad de tejido social.

El capitalismo previo a Hegel (sujeto de estudio de este artículo) muestra su posibilidad renovadora, una nueva centralidad para el ser humano, en donde las fuerzas productivas, comerciales y hasta exploradoras del mismo, comienzan a representar una mayor garantía para su reconocimiento económico y social, que los esquemas aristocráticos siempre defendidos por el feudalismo.

La comunicación, como ciencia y sistema, ha contribuido de manera fundamental a los procesos de consolidación del estado capitalista. Desde el ciclo de la comunicación como organizador y regulador, hasta los actuales procesos de posverdad, la ciencia de la comunicación es el gran ícono de sostén epistemológico del capitalismo actual.

1. 1. Comunicación y filosofía: primer desencuentro en el mundo occidental

Los procesos de comunicación, y las miradas filosóficas sobre la constitución y el ordenamiento de los grupos humanos, han tenido lugar, a lo largo del tiempo, distintos momentos álgidos.

El primero que esta investigación trae a colación es la guerra del Peloponeso, cuando las ciudades-estado griegas entraron en conflicto con Esparta, teniendo como escenario de guerra las ciudades e islas del sur de la actual Italia. En este ámbito, entraron en conflicto las posturas filosóficas y comunicacionales del mundo heleno, puesto que, era un sistema de valores los que ellos buscaban sostener y otros los mensajes que llegaban desde la metrópoli.

El punto de quiebre era que las tropas helenas reproducían el valor de la democracia entre hombres iguales y las decisiones en el campo de batalla se tomaban luego de profundas y amplias deliberaciones. Mientras que, en el campo espartano el mando era único, vertical, descendente y sin posibilidad de retroalimentación o discordia.

En el mundo occidental esta es la primera gran crisis entre los componentes filosóficos y los componentes comunicaciones de una sociedad organizada. Tarde y equívocamente llegaron las órdenes desde Atenas sobre verticalizar el mando y Esparta tuvo un triunfo contundente. Actualmente este conflicto es analizado minuciosamente en espacios académicos, políticos y militares.

1.2. Filosofía y comunicación en los albores renacentistas

Previamente al inicio de la totalidad eurocentrista, Francis Bacon, materialista-mecanicista inglés, fundamentó la necesidad de constituir estados que sean entes en donde los sistemas mecanicistas puedan funcionar con amplitud, claridad y canales completamente pre-estructurados. Esta postura, que busca establecer los espacios de encuentro entre comunicación y filosofía, es la evidencia de que Inglaterra (mucho antes de la revolución industrial) ya articulaba estructuras pre-capitalistas para buscar la finalización del modo de producción feudal.

Thomas Hobbes, es otro autor trascendente en el análisis de las sociedades humanas. Señalaba la importancia de la pérdida, en proporciones pequeñas, de la individualidad y libertad humanas, en beneficio de la construcción colectiva de un estado que garantizaría el ordenamiento jurídico y la protección integral de cada uno de sus miembros.

En Hobbes, se pre-configura que, para que ese estado logre convencer a sus miembros de esa renuncia de ciertas cuotas de libertad, iba a ser necesario un *sistema de persuasiones*. Es decir, se establece aquí la necesidad de una ciencia, que fortalezca las capacidades colaborativas entre individuos y un incipiente Estado.

Mientras lo anterior sucedía en Inglaterra, en la cuna del renacimiento (Italia), un autor condensaba y compilaba perspectivas conceptuales para la consolidación de la categoría Estado y la categoría Ciudad, como ejes sinérgicos, para la transición hacia el capitalismo, este autor, Nicolás Maquiavelo, expresaba la necesidad de que las recientes élites comerciales y mercantilistas, para su total triunfo económico, tendrían que derrotar a la estructura política feudal y establecer nuevas formas de control social y cultural con los habitantes de un grupo humano, haciendo menos visible la verticalidad y el tratamiento vasallo que imponían las clásicas visiones eurocentradas.

En el texto *El príncipe* de Maquiavelo (2002) se expresa:

> Debe tenerse en cuenta que no hay cosa más difícil de intentar, ni menos segura de conseguir, ni más peligrosa de manejar, que llegar a jefe o príncipe e imponer nuevas leyes. Porque serán enemigos suyos cuantos aman las viejas instituciones, y tibios amigos y defensores quienes aman las nuevas (p.47)

En esta cita de su libro clásico, Maquiavelo deja en manifiesto que el ejercicio del poder, y sobretodo de mantenerlo, tiene que ver con las formas en que ese poder establece relaciones con otras manifestaciones de liderazgo y con el pueblo en general.

Maquiavelo expresaba, la necesidad de que el jefe se muestre piadoso y a la vez severo, creyente en una fuerza divina pero a la vez autónomo en la toma de decisiones, con tacto para sus aliados y a la vez despiadado con enemigos y sobretodo con traidores.

Estos esquemas políticos, eran la consecuencia de una Europa que estaba dejando atrás, para siempre, el mundo feudal, y en esa transición hacia un sistema económico mucho más vertiginoso, mercantilista, comercial, se requería un ejercicio del poder no tan evidente, sino matizado con expresiones que, en la actualidad, se podrían definir como perspectivas de comunicación política.

En una Inglaterra, mucho más avanzada económica y políticamente, gracias a su pre-ilustración del siglo XVI, el teórico Tomás Moro, en su Tratado Principal, expone de manera novedosa, la intención de un salto para que la humanidad no atraviese la fase industrializada (ya eminente en ese entonces) logrando equilibrar una hermandad entre sus miembros a partir, no de esquemas de modernidad, sino de espacios de profunda comunicación humana. En el libro utopía, de Moro (1989) indica: "Los que viven juntos se ponen fácilmente de acuerdo en una forma de vida, y esto para la prosperidad de ambos pueblos, pues con sus leyes consiguen que todo sea suficiente y fructífero para todos" (p.65)

Este relato sobre una isla-ficción, retrata una perspectiva en que el autor de esta expresa su convencimiento de que la llegada de la industrialización iba a traer consigo los conflictos comunicacionales y la ausencia de paz. Propone, en su reemplazo, que la humanidad no transite por esas dinámicas económicas estructurales.

En las distintas manifestaciones del pensamiento europeo renacentista, existía, en la mayoría de los casos, un denominador común: un Estado que regula, ordena, establece la delimitación del accionar de sus habitantes en aras de la armonía y el equilibrio entre sus miembros.

Desde el racionalismo materialista, Baruch Spinoza interpretaba que la relación Estado- habitante, no podía, ni debía, tener la verticalidad que él creía habían sido expresadas antes por las anteriores escuelas filosóficas.

Spinoza (2014) en *El tratado teológico-político* manifiesta:

> La justicia e injusticia solo son concebibles en el Estado (...) Estado, como el derecho común determina qué es de éste y qué es del otro, se dice justo aquel que tiene una voluntad constante de dar a cada uno lo suyo, e injusto, por el contrario, aquel que se esfuerza en hacer suyo lo que es de otro (p. 97)

Spinoza cree posible que un Estado puede constituirse desde un ejercicio de generación permanente de hilos comunicantes con sus habitantes, logrando con ello una legitimación y respaldo de cada uno de los miembros de la colectividad. Spinoza manifiesta así, que en la posibilidad de que ese Estado tenga un carácter comunicante con sus actores, logrando con ello la visibilización de los sujetos, se alcanzará una subordinación voluntaria de los integrantes de una comunidad ante ese ente que los regula y los norma buscando siempre la justicia.

El empirismo inglés, también fundamentó, ya en el siglo XVIII, una interpretación del Estado que era coherente, con las formas del pensamiento empirista, que manifestaba la supremacía de la investigación sensorial por sobre el racionalismo continental europeo. En estas formas empíricas se critica por primera vez al Estado que se había consolidado en aquel entonces en Europa. Se fundamentaba la necesidad de que el Estado, en su propio seno, tenga los debidos contrapesos que permitan un ejercicio más regulado del poder. En el pensamiento filosófico, político y comunicacional del empirismo inglés, se hace hincapié en que la entrega de pequeñas cuotas de libertad humana para la consolidación del Estado, debían tener como justa reciprocidad, un Estado que auto-cuestione cada decisión y que genere espacios de retroalimentación y veeduría con sus habitantes.

En el libro *Segundo Tratado sobre el Gobierno Civil*, Locke (2004) argumenta:

> El único modo en que alguien se priva a sí mismo de su libertad natural y se somete a las ataduras de la sociedad civil es mediante un acuerdo con otros hombres (...) esto puede hacerlo cualquier grupo de hombres porque no desdeña la libertad de los demás, a quienes se deja, tal y como estaban, en estado de naturaleza (p. 97)

El autor reitera que el ejercicio sensorial del sujeto, para que sea una búsqueda experimental, requiere de las categorías de libertad e igualdad. Por lo que, la constitución de un Estado no puede basarse en otra máxima que no sea el respeto irrestricto a esa libertad humana, para que, partiendo de ello, los ciudadanos asuman la necesidad de una fuerza política que permita el ordenamiento jurídico y la convivencia de sus moradores.

1.3. Ilustración Francesa, consolidación del capitalismo, hegemonía del entre-Estado

La ilustración francesa manifiesta el carácter de la maduración del pensamiento liberal. A pesar de que las categorías de la Iglesia católica aún dominaban varios aspectos de la vida de los habitantes de Francia, el pensamiento filosófico y científico, ya impulsaban a un cambio radical de los paradigmas de la organización económica y social del país galo. Al visibilizar al poder clerical como una de las últimas formas del poder feudal, no poca de la producción filosófica de la ilustración francesa, fue en contra de la Iglesia. Otros de los valores que expresaron y socializaron los autores de esta escuela fue la universalización de la educación y la división de poderes del Estado (este último aún se mantiene con plena vigencia en el capitalismo occidental del siglo XXI).

Sus tres protagonistas más significativos fueron Voltaire, Montesquieu y Rousseau, este último en su libro *Contrato social* (2007) sostenía:

> Esta persona pública que así se forma, por la unión de los demás, tomaba en otro tiempo el nombre de ciudad y toma ahora el de *República* o de *cuerpo político*, que es llamado por sus miembros *Estado* (...) respecto a los asociados, toman colectivamente el nombre de *pueblo*, y se llaman en particular *ciudadanos*, cuanto son participantes de la autoridad soberana y súbditos, en cuanto sometidos a las leyes del Estado (pp. 46-47)

Desde este argumento la ilustración francesa manifestaba con mucha claridad que la forma fundamental de consolidación del Estado era a partir del desarrollo económico y material de sus habitantes. Habitantes que por primera vez se les asignaba la categoría de ciudadanos.

En la multidimensionalidad de su producción filosófica y en su propia transición, de un Empirismo alemán, a un Idealismo Trascendental, Inmanuel Kant desarrolló una destacada defensa del individuo, a quien no se le podía pedir ningún sacrificio en aras de un bienestar colectivo, no obstante, consideraba que el capitalismo, por sus posibilidades de intercambio mercantil, era el pilar fundamental para la paz mundial y el desarrollo de las sociedades. En su texto, *La paz perpetua*, Kant (2003) manifiesta:

> Un Estado no es un haber, un patrimonio. Es una sociedad de hombres sobre la cual nadie, sino ella misma puede mandar y disponer. Es un tronco con raíces propias; por consiguiente, incorporarlo a otro Estado, injertándolo, por decirlo así, en él, vale tanto como anular su existencia de persona moral y hacer de esta persona una cosa (p.3)

Kant prontamente observa una serie de conflictos entre los Estados que comienzan a desarrollarse en Europa. Revisaba que la supremacía comercial y financiera de un Estado iba a ser el mayor peligro para consolidar las relaciones igualitarias entre sus miembros. Junto a ello, Kant ponía hincapié en que esos Estados debían no solo permitir, sino garantizar la independencia de la actividad de los ciudadanos y la consolidación de una justicia que parta del ejercicio de ver por iguales a cada uno de los miembros de ese Estado.

1.4. Hegel, el Estado y la comunicación

Hegel, quien indiscutiblemente tributó al Idealismo alemán con sus conceptos sobre el *Absoluto*, tuvo en sus preceptos sobre el Estado, una dimensión completamente práctica y funcional a los ejercicios del poder establecidos en la Alemania de la época (Prusia).

Es muy común el axioma que indica que los alemanes piensan las revoluciones y los franceses las ejecutan. Bajo la premisa anterior, se puede analizar, los aportes teóricos sobre el Estado que expresó Hegel, a quienes no pocos lo denominan el primer y más fundamental filósofo del capitalismo occidental.

En su texto *filosofía del derecho*, Hegel (1975) plantea:

> Cuando la sociedad civil funciona sin trabas se produce dentro de ellas el progreso de la población y la industria (...) pero por otro lado (...) tiene como consecuencia la singularización y limitación del trabajo particular, y con ello, la dependencia y la miseria ligada a ese trabajo (...) la caída de una gran masa por debajo de un cierto nivel mínimo de subsistencia (...) lleva al surgimiento de una plebe, que por su parte proporciona la mayor facilidad para que se concentren en pocas manos riquezas desproporcionadas (p.274)

Hegel que expresaba que lo real era racional y lo racional a su vez real, creía que el Estado era el punto cúspide de esa racionalidad. Junto con la relación entre razón y realidad se suman la conciencia, tanto individual como colectiva. El Estado es el elemento que constituye la suma de esos tres componentes (razón-realidad-conciencia).

No obstante, Hegel (1975) ya visualiza que el desarrollo de los procesos industriales iban a generar una clase de seres humanos que estarían en la extrema miseria. Lo que representaba una amenaza para ese Estado, por lo que se debían analizar posibilidades mínimas de subsistencia para ese grupo humano. En el propio texto llega a indicar:

En su texto *filosofía del derecho*, Hegel (1975) plantea:

> El Estado es la realidad de la libertad concreta (...) el Estado es una voluntad divina, en cuanto a actual espíritu que se explica en forma real como una ordenación universal (...) el pueblo, considerado sin su monarca y sin la organización necesaria e inmediatamente conectiva de la totalidad, es la muchedumbre informe, que ya no es Estado, y a la cual ya no compete ninguna de las determinaciones que existen solamente en la totalidad formada en sí: soberanía, gobernación, jurisdicción, magistratura, clases y cualquier otra. (pp. 270-279).

Hegel deja asentado que es el Estado (como si fuera un ente del *Absoluto*), la única posibilidad para que el pueblo pueda articular la justicia porque en el Estado hay un *en sí* relacionado con lo correcto, con lo equitativo, con el beneficio colectivo, algo que los pueblos, en sí mismos están imposibilitados de articular.

Se trata de una relación en donde los seres humanos deben reconocer la superioridad del Estado puesto que el mismo es una fase suprema que se piensa y se manifiesta para que los intereses individuales no se contrapongan con el desarrollo colectivo.

En libro *filosofía de la historia*, Hegel (2008) argumenta:

> La primera exteriorización de un Estado es autoritaria e instintiva. También la ecuación de obediencia y poder o de temor y gobernante, implican una relación de voluntad. Semejante composición de factores se suele encontrar ya en estados primitivos en que la voluntad específica de los individuos no tiene vigencia (...) se renuncia la manifestación de lo particular y que la voluntad general se convierta en lo esencial. Esta unidad de lo general y lo individual es la idea que se hace presente como Estado y que luego se desarrolla cada vez más. (p. 45).

En esta reflexión Hegel observa que los grupos humanos que asumieron la necesidad de constituir voluntades generales colectivas fueron los que más prontamente tuvieron un desarrollo integral y que esos mismos procesos mostraron la necesidad de que el *en sí* del individuo necesitaba menguarse a favor del Estado.

No solamente el alcance de una libertad del individuo (que se lo logra con el capitalismo) sino que es la maduración subjetiva de la libertad humana. En este sentido, en el Estado, el ser humano encuentra garantías para su desarrollo racional, protección de los peligros de la barbarie, y también posibilidad de expresar sus más amplias manifestaciones subjetivas, logrando con ello el pleno desarrollo de sus dimensiones científicas, filosóficas, artísticas y sociales.

Es neurálgico señalar que en la Alemania de aquella época no existía un quiebre político entre la monarquía (aristocracia) y la burguesía (élite comercial). Se había logrado una alianza ampliada en que las ambas partes señaladas lograron articular un Estado que atendía las exigencias de las élites y contenía las amenazas de la insurgencia de los menos favorecidos.

Otra de las premisas fundamentales era la necesidad de que los ciudadanos y la sociedad civil en su conjunto asuman una total confianza en el Estado, puesto que eso iba a permitir la optimización del tiempo y recursos para que sea necesario articular procesos de legitimación permanente.

Vale indicar que Hegel, mucho antes de Karl Marx, hablaba de superestructuras y de poderes de una gran fuerza que determinarían la propia organización del Estado (poder financiero, élites económicas, etc.).

En el libro *filosofía real*, Hegel (2006) sustenta:

> El poder del Estado interviene y tiene que saltar a la palestra para velar por la conservación de cada esfera (...) la *libertad de la industria* debe ser respetada, por consiguiente, la intervención del Estado tiene que ser tan discreta como posible (...) el poder del Estado es la visión del conjunto (...) las ramas de la industria se abandonan sin necesidad de que intervenga el Estado, pero sacrificando la generación presente y aumentando la pobreza. Por eso son precisas las tasas de pobres e instituciones de asistencia social. (p. 199)

Hegel establece la libertad autónoma de la clase industrial para permitir que la misma sea un ente protagónico del desarrollo económico de un Estado. Asume como inevitable y fatalidad histórica el surgimiento de la pobreza, haciendo énfasis que es el Estado el que tendrá que articular espacios de asistencia para no permitir que la plebe se subleve. Bajo esa égida el Estado tiene que generar espacios de colaboración con los menos favorecidos, y por consiguiente, esquematizar un aparato ideológico que le permita, desde las simbologías, que esos grupos más vulnerables no se subleven contra el orden y poder establecidos.

En el libro Hegel, interpretaciones fenomenológicas, Fink (2011) afirma:

> Lo universal en forma de pueblo de la sustancia ética reúne en sí a los individuos, pero de tal manera que estos mismos se abran a lo universal y que en su obrar e impulsar efectúan lo que la ética universal es. Los individuos están en el pueblo, no a modo de piedras en un montón (...) sino que obran el impulso universal con conciencia y reconociendo la ética. Viven en la medida en que se 'universalizan'. Los individuos se saben como tales porque están abiertos al todo del pueblo y a su mundo espiritual (...) Hegel caracteriza la relación entre individuo y pueblo como un estar mutuamente entretejido el uno con el otro. El individuo lleva a cabo su praxis vital en la medida en que ante todo satisface sus necesidades vitales como ser natural. Necesita alimento, vestido, hogar (...) el individuo se comporta ya de modo universal cuando se busca a sí mismo y busca su beneficio (p. 391)

Este filósofo contemporáneo reflexiona sobre la obra de Hegel, dejando en claro que el individuo, desde el propio Hegel, tiene un protagonismo activo e influyente en la participación de ese Estado. Se establece una diferencia fundamental entre individuo y pueblo que tiene que ver con el accionar de ambos, sin embargo, hay un reflejo mutuo, puesto que el campo ético desde donde se piensan tiene que ver con la convivencia pacífica. Desde esta definición, que es fundamentalmente capitalista, se entiende que el individuo colabora con las categorías de *lo universal* solamente en la medida en que ese Estado le permite alcanzar sus necesidades y satisfacciones. Esto, lejos de ser criticado por Fink, es entendido a la altura de categoría ética.

En el capítulo Hegel, dialéctica del amo y el esclavo del libro la filosofía y el barro de la historia, Feinmann (2008) define:

> Hegel que viene a expresar un *poder total*, tiene que instaurar un *saber total* (...) La burguesía con su revolución se ha apoderado de la *cosa en sí*. También debe hacerlo la filosofía que debe a acceder a un conocimiento de la totalidad. Nada debe escapar ahora al poder del sujeto (...) Hegel quiere pensar toda la historia, pero tiene que hacerlo partiendo de un sujeto. Este sujeto debe ser universal. Entramos a la infinitud de la razón que define sustancialmente, a la filosofía de Hegel (p. 107)

En este aporte conceptual, Hegel retrata a una burguesía que ha dejado atrás finalmente al poder feudal y que, en su alcance comercial del mundo, requiere sustancialmente que sus principios económicos logren una globalidad de manera que se pueda establecer relaciones jurídicas, mercantiles, financieras, en la integralidad mundial, para así esquematizar las nuevas relaciones socio-productivas del capitalismo triunfante.

El aporte del Estado a estos procesos de *Totalidad* y *Globalidad* están relacionados con la mayor colaboración tributaria posible de ese Estado a esas industrias y con el poder mediador que debe auto exigirse ese Estado en cualquier proceso de contraposiciones entre las élites industriales y la sociedad civil.

Hegel entonces, al hablar sobre el Estado, entiende que el sujeto histórico no está en inferioridad de condiciones con relación a ese constructo, sino que, el Estado es la suma de las razones objetivas y subjetivas, que le permiten a la sociedad capitalista articularse como fuerza motora de crecimiento económico.

El Estado en Hegel, a partir de la conformación de instituciones, organismos, y espacios de mediación, logra que los antagonismos y las contraposiciones de sus sujetos, no amenacen la institucionalidad y el sistema de crecimiento económico. Para Hegel, por primera vez en la historia, la humanidad había alcanzado un modo de producción que permitía a todos los seres humanos, lograr cualquier meta económica que se autoimpusieran.

Este axioma hegeliano, de indiscutible defensa del progreso económico que supuestamente el capitalismo ofrece a cada sujeto, ha demostrado en la actualidad su inconsistencia, puesto que no solamente entre sujetos, sino que además entre Estados, son cada vez más visibles las diferencias económicas, de soberanía alimentaria, de acceso a la salud, de estar integrados en sistemas de educación eficientes, entre otras grandes disparidades que continúan dos siglos después de los postulados hegelianos.

Schopenhauer, entre numerosas oposiciones con el pensar hegeliano, considera que la realidad presente, cotidiana, poco tiene que ver con la razón, por lo que denuncia, prontamente que esa razón es capaz de ajustar a la realidad ¿bajo qué mecanismo? El Estado.

Sostiene que la libertad no puede articularse desde un marco de sometimiento de parte de la razón (que opera desde el Estado) hacía los individuos (que ven condicionadas sus posibilidades, su libertad, y su Voluntad/Representación). La libertad, como ente condicionada por la razón, más precisamente, condicionada por la dialéctica hegeliana, es fundamental para entender las contraposiciones entre ambos teóricos.

El Estado no solo que poco puede hacer para evitar los conflictos entre sus integrantes, sino que requiere de la injusticia para auto legitimarse como ente de regulación.

Es enemigo del Ser, porque es contraria a los esquemas de Voluntad/Representación en el sujeto. Además, el individuo, no se encuentra en plenitud en las dinámicas de la razón, sino que él es profundamente intuitivo, busca continuidades, conexiones interiores, causas personales con los fenómenos que se le presentan, antes que entrar a procesos de complejidad abstracta para explicar el mundo.

1.5. La comunicación como ciencia de la organización, globalización y totalización del capitalismo

La comunicación tiene su fase de expresión de desarrollo como disciplina, con sus respectivos objetos de estudio a mediados del siglo XIX. Esto se debe a que, indiscutiblemente, las ciencias de la comunicación nacen a la par del triunfo del capitalismo global y como intento de acompañamiento a las nuevas fases de desarrollo económico del mundo occidental.

Este artículo establece cuatro momentos de las ciencias de la comunicación en su ejercicio de acompañar al nuevo modo de producción reinante, y son:

- Comunicación como elemento de organización social (1870-1920)

- Comunicación y análisis de las masas (1920-1960)

- Comunicación como fenómeno global y alcance mediático (1960-1990)

- Comunicación como expresión de totalidad, cosificación y generador de pos-verdades (1990-actualidad)

Comunicación como elemento de organización social (1870-1920)

La comunicación como parte tributante de la organización social, es expresada en la analogía de lo biológico que compara el sistema del cuerpo humano con la conformación de las sociedades modernas. Por lo cual, autores como Aguste Comte, Herbert Spencer, entre otros, manifestaron que la comunicación equivalía a la sangre humana, es decir, distribuía y regulaba la actividad social, permitiendo así el desarrollo de las fuerzas productivas del capitalismo europeo occidental de fines del siglo XIX.

Este enfoque mecanicista entendía la comunicación más como una herramienta que como un sistema, fue abordado no solamente en las ciencias sociales más tradicionales, sino también en los enfoques económicos y psicológicos de la época.

Así, la sociedad industrial llegaba a encarar a la sociedad orgánica y la tarea de la comunicación era contribuir a lo que Herbert Spencer denominó el "sistema nervioso social" (Medios de comunicación, primeras investigaciones, encuestas).

Este enfoque, en el inicio del siglo XX y en la primera guerra mundial, supuso el fin de su vigencia.

Comunicación y análisis de las masas (1920-1960)

El Capitalismo comenzaba a sufrir sus primeras crisis globales, a base de ello las ciencias de la comunicación comenzaron la construcción y el perfeccionamiento de la propaganda. La misma constituía un medio mucho más eficiente, económico y pacífico que la violencia. El objetivo central era alcanzar el favor del pueblo, asumido aquí como masas, puesto que estaba impedido de una reflexión crítica de los contenidos que le llegaban construidos para alcanzar un dominio de la subjetividad de los sujetos.

Mattelart (1997) especifica la forma teórica-metodológica en que lo esquemas comunicacionales tributan al fortalecimiento del capitalismo.

En su texto, *La historia de las teorías de la comunicación*, detalla:

> Según Laswell el proceso de comunicación cumple tres funciones (...): a) la vigilancia del entorno, revelando todo lo que podría amenazar (...) al sistema de valores de una comunidad (...); b) la puesta en relación de los componentes de la sociedad para producir una respuesta al entorno; c) la transmisión de la herencia social. (...) Lazarsfeld y Merton añaden (...) una cuarta: el entretenimiento. (...) Las funciones como consecuencias que contribuyen a la adaptación (...) Las funciones impiden que las disfunciones precipiten la crisis del sistema (p.31)

Desde esta perspectiva, los teóricos de este enfoque (Lasswell, Lazarsfeld, Merton) establecían las funciones básicas que debían desarrollar los procesos comunicacionales en su relación con las masas. Las que eran:

a. Vigilancia del entorno

b. Relación para generar respuestas

c. Transmisión de la herencia social

d. Entretenimiento

La comunicación, ciencia de ordenamiento, regulación y flujo en el capitalismo del siglo XIX, tuvo en el siglo XX la tarea de generar esquemas que permitan a las masas (no públicos desde el funcionalismo mecanicista) adherirse a los postulados más globales de la ideología de un Estado. Este Estado respondía a los interés corporativistas o en ocasiones era el principal protagonista (y castrador) de todo el tejido social. En el siglo XXI, con los desafíos que representan las redes sociales, la comunicación, y sobre todo sus compañías tradicionales, siguen reflexionando su rol en los tiempos de imperios comunicacionales y pos verdad.

Algunos de los autores de esta perspectiva creían que estos componentes de los medios de comunicación masiva (MCM) iban a permitir el fortalecimiento de la democracia y la sociedad. Pero el contexto económico de crisis global y la pronta llegada de la crisis política (que culminaría en la segunda guerra mundial), motivó a un uso funcionalista de estas formas de expresión con que los MCM interpretaban a la sociedad y simbolizaban al capitalismo en general.

Comunicación como fenómeno global y alcance mediático (1960-1990)

En este ciclo temporal, las ciencias de la comunicación, y especialmente, los MCM alcanzaron una globalidad total y una credibilidad que les permitían generar opinión pública y una influencia en la interpretación de cada uno de los saberes ciudadanos y de sus manifestaciones políticas y sociales. No es vano, esta perspectiva inicia con la declarada batalla por el espacio entre los dos protagonistas de la guerra fría (entre Estados Unidos y la Unión Soviética) y culmina con la caída del muro de Berlín y el triunfo hegemónico del capitalismo (1990).

Los medios de comunicación son un actor más que protagónico en el marco de este conflicto filosófico, tanto es así que en varias ocasiones, especialistas de las áreas disciplinarias como la sociología, antropología y comunicología, determinan que el triunfo de un imperio por encima de otro (Estados Unidos sobre la Unión soviética) fue una victoria ideológica. El mayor sustento de esta definición es la famosa frase desarrollada por el filósofo del pentágono Francis Fukuyama, cuando exclamó "es el fin de la historia", aclamando con ello, el fin de categorías como totalidad, globalidad y decretando (vanamente) la muerte filosófica de Hegel. Lo que en términos de interrelación comunicacional puede interpretarse como una terrible injusticia puesto que fue precisamente Hegel quien mejor conceptualizó, desde la filosofía, la necesidad de la globalidad capitalista.

Comunicación como expresión de totalidad, cosificación y generador de pos-verdades (1990-actualidad)

En esta fase aún vigente de las ciencias de la comunicación, se establece a esta disciplina como autora de saberes y generadora, ya no solamente de agendas temáticas y esquemas mediáticos sino, sorprendentemente, de realidades, de verdades y de interpretaciones hegemónicas y universales.

En El sujeto absoluto comunicacional del libro La filosofía y el barro de la historia, Feinmann (2008) sustenta:

No hay subjetividades autónomas. El sujeto absoluto comunicacional sujeta a los hombres de hoy. Les hace ver lo que hay que ver. Hablar de lo que hay que hablar. Coloniza sus conciencias. Impide el más mínimo surgimiento de pensamiento crítico (...) ¿Puede haber libertad de prensa en un mundo en que lo informático se ha monopolizado? ¿Hay verdades o el vértigo comunicacional las ahoga? Los sujetos viven agotados de informaciones pero no tienen ninguna sola verdad (...) El poder de los *mass media*, a través de las políticas de fusión es expansivo en la actualidad. Ese poder es *uno* e intenta someter a lo *múltiple*. Y lo somete. Ya no existe lo *múltiple*. Lo que existe es el poder de lo *uno comunicacional*. Ese poder se dirige hacia el sometimiento, hacia el avasallamiento, hacia muy especialmente el *aturdimiento* de las conciencias. El mundo hace ruido. *Todo es ruido*". (p. 789).

Esta definición, a la que los autores del artículo se subscriben, se la puede abordar desde las posibilidades que tienen los imperios mediáticos para generar y cosificar la verdad desde que Bourdieu escribió el texto *la guerra del golfo no ha tenido lugar* hasta los estudios contemporáneos sobre la post-verdad, se muestra que la comunicación en la actualidad ya no se conforma con ser la generadora funcional de los esquemas de regulación sino que es, en el presente, el protagonista fundamental del esquema capitalista y el generador y reproductor, no solamente de saberes, sino que además, de las interpretaciones culturales e identitarias de los espacios de reproducción social en cada rincón del mundo actual.

Conclusiones

Hegel indica que el capitalismo ordena el progreso humano y las teorías funcionalistas de comunicación precisan que para ordenar ese progreso humano está la comunicación. Es decir, por una parte, Hegel manifiesta que el capitalismo es el devenir máximo del desarrollo social y al mismo tiempo, la comunicación es una herramienta, un sistema de flujos, un canal que contribuye a esos procesos.

La filosofía del siglo XX quiere dejar a un lado los sistemas filosóficos globales, de alguna manera, dejar a Hegel atrás, por eso funciona el lenguaje. La comunicación entonces deja de servir como una herramienta de organización industrial sino de adherencia a la propaganda para abrazar el discurso ideológico de la estructura gobernante y de las élites económicas que generan agenda social.

En el siglo XXI la filosofía se enfrenta al fin del postmodernismo con la caída de las torres gemelas y busca la construcción de un posthumanismo. Entonces, la comunicación puede servir como una ciencia de empoderamiento ciudadano en donde los actores sociales pueden construir relatos de interpretación social, lo que redunda en el desafío de la postverdad de estos tiempos.

Referencias bibliográficas

Feinmann, J. (2008) La filosofía y el barro de la historia. Buenos Aires: Editorial Planeta.

Fink, E. (2011) Hegel, interpretaciones fenomenológicas. Barcelona: Herder Editorial.

Hegel, G. (2008) filosofía de la historia. Buenos Aires: Editorial Claridad.

Hegel, G. (2006) filosofía real. Madrid: Fondo de Cultura Económica de España.

Hegel, G. (1975) Filosofía del derecho. Buenos Aires: Editorial Sudamericana.

Kant, I. (2003) La paz perpetua. Buenos Aires: Biblioteca Virtual Universal.

Locke, J. (2004) Segundo Tratado sobre el Gobierno Civil. Madrid: Alianza Editorial.

Maquiavelo, N. (2002). El Príncipe. Capítulo VI. Barcelona: Editorial Planeta.

Mattelart, A. (1997) La historia de las teorías de comunicación. Barcelona: Editorial Paidós Comunicación.

Moro, T. (1989). Utopía. Barcelona: Casa Editoria Bosch.

Rousseau, J. (2007). Contrato social. Madrid: Espasa.

Spinoza, B. (2014). Tratado Teológico-Político. Madrid: Alianza editorial.

EL NUEVO PARADIGMA DE TURISMO AMBIENTAL Y EL PROBLEMA DE LA COMUNICACIÓN EN EL TURISMO

Ingeniero António Santos Veloso
Centro de Formación de Profesores (Profesional) de Conimbriga

PhD António Dos Santos Queirós
Centro de Filosofía de la Universidad de Lisboa

Resumen

Identificación del problema y estableciendo del tema

El Turismo Ambiental como un concepto de turismo sostenible que valora y promueve la conservación del patrimonio de interés para la sostenibilidad del turismo y su organización en rutas y circuitos El papel esencial de los guías turísticos para una mayor valoración de los patrimonios que pueden y deben despertar en los turistas un interés duradero. La subestimación del tema de la comunicación en el turismo: *why?*, ¿por qué?

Los pasos metodológicos

Para analizar el tema, que es vasto y complejo, en el contexto de un artículo científico, seleccionamos un problema clave: Lo papel del guía en el sistema de comunicación de turismo (ambiental), en el marco de la competición entre dos paradigmas principales de la filosofía aplicada al turismo: el hedonista y el ambientalista.

Los modelos de guionamento en confronto y los atributos intrínsecos del discurso del guía del turismo ambiental

Además de los conocimientos científicos y técnicos indispensables al trabajo del guía, analizaremos la importancia de los principios del Código Mundial de la Ética del Turismo y los principios de recuperación y conservación del patrimonio (s), a partir de las resoluciones de las Conferencias Mundiales de las Naciones Unidas sobre el Medio Ambiente y sobre el Patrimonio; pero iremos más allá, cuestionando el concepto de Guionamento como un arte de desempeño que oriente los turistas para las experiencias apropiadas a sus características y de los patrimonios que van a visitar, reforzando el disfrute de sus valencias culturales.

Conclusiones

Llegamos entonces a los resultados sobre el perfil científico, técnico y ético del guía de turismo ambiental y discutiremos no solamente los componentes de su discurso y su narrativa, así como el recorrido de su formación, con el objetivo de promover sus requisitos de guía del turismo ambiental y satisfacer las necesidades del cambio de paradigma hacia el turismo ambiental.

Palabras clave

Paradigma. Comunicación. Turismo. Ambiental. Ética. Desempeno

1. Introducción. Ética y turismo. Primero enfoque metodológico[14]

Suponiendo que el lector de los temas del turismo no está familiarizado con el pensamiento ambiental y la reflexión de la filosofía ambiental, es necesario introducir en el análisis algunas referencias filosóficas y una breve reseña sobre la nueva visión de las relaciones entre naturaleza y cultura en la óptica de la filosofía ambiental.

Algunos autores implicados en la investigación sobre ética y Turismo proponen tres paradigmas con particular relevancia a este tema:

> "...the Aristotelian paradigm of virtue ethics, eudaimonia; the Kantian paradigm of the categorical imperative respect for the person and the paradigm of the utilitarian ethics considering the greatest good". (Jamal and Menzel, 2011)

Esta perspectiva científica y ética continúa siendo exclusivamente humanista.

En el libro *The Imperative of Responsibility. In Search of an Ethics for the Technological Age* el autor, judío alemán emigrado a Canadá y Estados Unidos, dado la tremenda influencia de la técnica moderna sobre la naturaleza, formula un nuevo imperativo categórico para la acción del hombre, más allá del imperativo kantiano de conformar los actos del individuo con el principio de una ley universal. Y dibuja un nuevo marco ético que resulta de la necesidad de establecer la conducta humana dentro de los límites que salvaguardan la continuidad de la vida y su diversidad:

> "Act so that the effects of your action are compatible with the permanence of genuine human life. (Jonas, 1979)

Según este principio ético estamos en lo límite del humanismo, pero no cruzamos aun la frontera del antropocentrismo.

La filosofía de la naturaleza y la filosofía del medio ambiente hizo posible construir una nueva ontología crítica del antropocentrismo, una nueva epistemología, fundado en la crítica del etnocentrismo y una nueva ética, como teoría moral del valor universal y contenido práctico aplicable a todos los dominios sociales. Esta es la opinión del autor responsable contra la opinión prevaleciente en el campo de la filosofía, que

---

[14] El lector interesado en estos temas puede encontrar en el *International Journal of Scientific Management and Tourism. iManagement and Tourism* un ensayo más desarrollado y otros artículos, todavía más focalizados en el turismo que en la filosofía y comunicación. Consultar bibliografía.

considera que el foro de ética de la conciencia individual y por lo tanto no puede tener valor universal!

Como en la filosofía de Espinosa y después en la de los filósofos ambientalistas, el impulso fundamental de la filosofía ambiental fueran los problemas éticos y los problemas morales.

El esfuerzo por distinguir los conceptos de ética y moral, ética normativa (Qué debo hacer?) del concepto filosófico o *meta-ethics* (Qué es la naturaleza del bien), no es simple. Si la ética normativa es lo que la gente común entiende por "ética" y *meta-ethics* (meta ética) puede ser lo que para el sentido común significa la moralidad...esta visión conjunta se queda en el marco de la visión antropocéntrica de estos problemas. Todavía, la verdad es que en el último siglo la reflexión moral se reorientó para un *nuevo foco, el medio ambiente.*

La ética ambiental se desarrolló en dos ramas principales: *Biocentrism,* una teoría universal sobre el valor moral intrínseco de todos los seres, que por lo tanto, requieren el nuestro respeto. Y la ética de la comunidad biótica, el *Ecocentrism*:

> "how Nature can be a community of which we are members, and in within which it is possible for us to conduct ourselves well. (Leopold, 1947)...

...pero también la *deep ecology* (ecologia radical) y así sucesivamente.

La ética ambiental, en nuestra visión filosófica, está apoyada en dos principios _ la crítica del antropocentrismo y la crítica del etnocentrismo. Es su finalidad dar una respuesta universal a los problemas fundamentales de nuestro tiempo: la crisis ambiental, social, económico y político, que es representada por lo amenaza que plantea la guerra nuclear y las armas de destrucción masiva; es también su finalidad contribuir a cambiar la forma de las actividades humanas insostenibles, en todas las áreas; tal fue el caso de la bioética en el campo de la salud y, más tarde, la ciencia y la política y por último, en el turismo.

La moral, en nuestra perspectiva filosófica, es siempre una expresión y representación determinadas por el contexto histórico y la dominación social, lo que le concede un carácter sectario. Necesitamos de una teoría moral que pueda venir a ser universal y atemporal (diseñado en el presente y en el futuro), capaces de orientar la conducta individual, la ciencia y las ideologías políticas, pero que no considere el hombre como el producto final de la evolución de la vida.

La biodiversidad de la Vida con la Vida Humana, sólo representa la cumbre actual de la evolución compleja del Cosmos, pero no sabemos si nuestra especie, nacida en la Tierra, representa el enlace final de la evolución cosmológica. Así el imperativo ético para preservar la vida y no sólo el hombre y conservar la Vida antes del Hombre y la Tierra, cuna de la vida cósmica y por ahora la única cuna, debe ganar moral fuerza en las sociedades humanas.

El Hombre es depredador y creador de nuevos biotopos y siendo en la actualidad la forma más compleja de la vida, su extinción podría bloquear la expansión de la diversidad, para qué y en esta perspectiva el Humanismo moral regresa al centro de la filosofía ambiental y de ética ambiental.[15]

Para buscar una respuesta a estas cuestiones, nasció una nueva perspectiva ética, una teoría construida sobre los principios (meta-ética, que definen la naturaleza del bien), aplicable a todas las actividades humanas (las éticas prácticas que configuran la moral social y las deontologías), incluyendo las actividades turísticas.

El concepto de Valor en la economía del patrimonio

La lectura y la interpretación del paisaje son la base para la creación del producto turístico y la primera metamorfosis del valor. Es el "la ecología del paisaje" y su "metafísica", que constituyen la esencia del recurso turístico, pero sólo su interpretación y lectura producen un incremento de valor cultural y económico. El paisaje no es un libro abierto, inteligible empíricamente. La suya transformación en producto turístico pasa por su legibilidad, lo que le da un valor de uso; Es una metamorfosis que, en términos de la economía genera valor, y es también un proceso de alfabetización cultural, mediado por la construcción de la lenguaje de comunicación turística; el resultado de este proceso cambia la forma y la esencia de los conceptos tradicionales del recurso y del producto turísticos.

La Historia Natural, servido por las Ciencias de la Tierra, la Geología y la Geomorfología en particular, revelan la diversidad del patrimonio geológico y sus monumentos naturales. El profesor Galopim de Carvalho[16] propone, en este sentido, la clasificación de tres tipos de Geo monumentos: afloramientos, sitios y paisajes, en conformidad con una creciente dimensión física.

Las Ciencias de la Vida, nos informan de las dimensiones y el valor de la biodiversidad, especialmente la Biología y la Botánica, así como sobre el

---

[15] Es este imperativo ético que reintegra al hombre en la naturaleza sin estado de dominio que la *deep ecology* y los radicales desprecian.
[16] Consultar Galopim de Carvalho, A. M., Queirós, A. (1999) Geomonumentos.

valor de los nuevos biotopos que resultan de la humanización del paisaje. La Historia social en sus valencias arqueológicas, etnográficas y artísticas, nos permite disfrutar del patrimonio construido, obras de arte y literatura y de los objetos y piezas etnográficas.

Y cuando hablamos de estas "materias primas", no olvidamos la dimensión inmaterial, su traducción en los imaginarios clásico y popular y en sus expresiones creativas, en la literatura, en la danza, en lo filosofar, en la música...

La expansión de la especie humana por todas las regiones del mundo y su adaptación a la diversidad de hábitat ha generado en la edad moderna una nueva la relación de la humanidad con la naturaleza: dejaran de existir los marcos naturales puros, todo el paisaje se convierte, directamente o indirectamente, por la actividad humana, produciendo un sin nombre de destrucción pero también nuevos paisajes culturales.

El capital turístico no se constituí solamente con la inversión en bienes inmobiliarios y en equipamientos del turismo (capital fijo) y en capital variable (materias primas tradicionales, salarios de técnicos y trabajadores especializados)..., pero cada vez más con la adición de inversión intelectual, científica y cultural (más allá de la planificación, gestión y marketing), en lo proceso de creación de productos turísticos como son los productos del turismo cultural, del turismo de naturaleza (o ecoturismo)y del turismo en espacio rural.

Los conceptos de Ruta y Circuito, basados en los paisajes culturales

Los conceptos de Ruta y Circuito de turismo se fundan en la necesidad de utilizar una metodología científica interdisciplinaria y multidisciplinaria para interpretar y organizar la visita al territorio, que permite leer e interpretar los paisajes culturales, rurales y urbanos.

La primera clave de esta lectura y interpretación es la Historia Natural, son las Ciencias de la Tierra, como la Geología. De pronto seguidas por las Ciencias de Vida, que revelan el esplendor de la biodiversidad. Y es la Historia social y artística, asociada con la Etnografía y la Antropología.

Pero probablemente, la Geografía es la ciencia que, en su metodología de trabajo científico es más cercana de las «Ciencias de Turismo» de trabajo. Como esta ciencia, la esencia de la metodología de trabajo científico de la información y guionamento del turismo consiste en 'describir e interpretar' la Tierra y los hombres que viven en su seno, pero de forma accesible a los diferentes segmentos del público y, por aquí, pasa la separación entre el objeto científico y el producto turístico, el recorrido científico y la Ruta y sus Circuitos del Turismo.

Esta concepción científica mientras que conduce a una filosofía nacida de la observación y lectura del paisaje y de la síntesis de la tierra y del hombre que habita y transforma el paisaje (lo que llamamos 'paisaje cultural'), mientras que la amenaza degradar o destruir, justifica la necesidad de una ética del turismo, construida como las nueva Éticas Ambientales, mediante la crítica del antropocentrismo y del etnocentrismo.

Entendemos por Ruta de Turismo un conjunto organizado de Circuitos de descubrimiento y disfrute de todos los patrimonios, con una identidad propia y única, fundada en la ecología del paisaje y en la metafísica del paisaje[17], accesible a todos los públicos pero con productos diferenciados según sus segmentos, potenciadores de la organización y desarrollo de las Cadenas de Valor de la actividad turística.

Definimos Circuito Turístico como un recorrido integrador de todos los patrimonios, de corta duración (no debe superar un día), accesible a todos los públicos pero segmentado, con una identidad autónoma y inconfundible, organizado desde la perspectiva de descubrimiento y disfrute de la ecología del paisaje (en el sentido de contribución científica interdisciplinaria para su lectura) y de la metafísica del paisaje (patrimonio inmaterial, imaginario clásico y popular), en conformidad con el principio de "comunicacional/ emocional de la "montaje de atracciones ", capaz de sostener y desarrollar las Cadenas de Valor del turismo.

Aunque hay elementos comunes entre los Circuitos _ por ejemplo, las iglesias de la misma época, comunes platos gastronómicos, la misma flora... la suma de su patrimonio debe producir dialécticamente una oferta única y identitaria. Y es también por eso que la actividad turística es diferente de otros dominios científicos, la selección y valoración es determinada por la diferenciación del producto de turismo.

Este nuevo concepto de Circuito es construido con los aportes conceptuales de la Geografía, "observación selectiva y significativa" del paisaje cultural, es decir, de su patrimonio histórico, natural, etnográfico; de la Filosofía de la Naturaleza y del Medio Ambiente, "ecología del paisaje y metafísica del paisaje"; de las Ciencias de la Comunicación, incluyendo la Psicología de los afectos y del cine ("el montaje de atracciones es un concepto eisensteiniano); de la Economía Política, las "Cadenas de Valor". Y su construcción metodológica consiste en la reapropiación por un nuevo objeto de estudio (el Turismo, en el marco de las Ciencias del Turismo) de los conceptos tradicionalmente utilizados en otros dominios científicos.

---

[17] Patrimonio material (tangible) y inmaterial (intangible) del paisaje, dimensión física y metafísica del paisaje.

2. Objetivos Generales y Específicos. Segundo enfoque metodológico. Cuadro de intervención y conceptos fundamentales del guionamento en turismo

Para discutir el papel que actualmente debe asignarse al Guía, contemplando la conservación y valoración del patrimonio tangible e intangible, donde resultará un cuadro referente a sus maestrías personales y competencias profesionales, tenemos que considerar lo que creemos que debe entenderse por recursos potenciales de patrimonio para convertirse en productos turísticos. Por las razones que vamos a exponer y discutir en este texto, consideramos imprescindible observar en la comunicación de la actividad turística las siguientes ideas o condiciones

1. La estrategia de planificación, organización y gestión del turismo moderno debe estar conectada con el desarrollo sostenible y con el Código Mundial de Ética para el Turismo.

2. El paisaje cultural, ya sea rural o urbano, constituí un recurso turístico potencialmente transformable en producto turístico. Pero el paisaje se vuelve efectivamente un producto turístico con el nivel correspondiente al su valor real y su visita solamente creará disfrute y significará placer, si incorporar una adecuada interpretación (que no es sólo ver sino también sentir, oír... debe ser multisensorial), indispensable para agregar un nuevo valor cultural y económico a la actividad de visitar el patrimonio.

3. Esta interpretación debe considerar la cuestión del gusto, intrínsecamente vinculado a la cuestión de los valores y por lo tanto a la ética y a la moral social y a la estética. La difusión de los valores de la Ética Ambiental y los valores de su filosofía de la naturaleza y del medio ambiente, causaron también un cambio sustancial en el concepto de calidad del producto turístico, certificado de valores que ahora se valora cuando tiene un certificado ambiental, ambiente, no solamente en su material pero también en su dimensión inmaterial.

4. El Turismo Cultural y el Turismo de Naturaleza, incluyendo el Turismo en los Espacios Rurales, tres categorías diferenciadas por sus estructuras orgánicas y distintos productos, pero mui cerca, integran un único concepto, el Turismo Ambiental, porque el concepto de ambiente corresponde a los de naturaleza más cultura; en nuestra época toda la naturaleza ha sufrido la influencia del hombre. Los productos del turismo ambiental

tienden a predominar en el gusto de la clase media, integrando el patrimonio material y el patrimonio inmaterial. Y para obtener los efectos deseados de la lectura, comprensión y experiencia por parte del visitante, el guionamento debe integrar la ecología del paisaje (patrimonio material) y su metafísica (patrimonio inmaterial), que constituyen la esencia del producto turístico.

Los límites de las nuevas tecnologías y la importancia estratégica de información y guionamento por el Guía Turístico

Únicamente el guionamento hecho por un guía profesional cualificado y conocedor del patrimonio permite combinar la información personalizada y la información por la tecnología para lograr comunicación, que quiere decir:

- Hacer una presentación adaptada a los destinatarios: a su generación, educación, cultura y gusto;

- Ayudar cada visitante a ir haciendo la interpretación y disfrute del producto, no utilizando el Guía su autoridad profesional, pero si una información sugestiva, empática, y respondiendo a las preguntas o hipótesis formuladas por el visitante. Por supuesto esta calidad del guionamento también tiene que ver con el tamaño, comportamiento y uniformidad del grupo. Y puede mostrar bajo qué circunstancias la visita en grupo tendrá mayor calidad;

- Aprovechar los momentos de mayor placer que pueden ser proporcionados por los patrimonios_ o las narrativas asociadas, un detalle, una historia, un mito, un leyenda_ patrimonio como escenario o, más correctamente, como el personaje principal del momento de la visita que se convirtió en una escena dramatizada;

- Únicamente con el contacto personal puede funcionar la empatía, la capacidad para motivar la audición y la interpretación dialogante que son aspectos que aumentan el disfrute transformando recursos en productos turísticos. También se trata de la única forma de embarcarse en interpretaciones más complejas, admisibles sólo cuando los interlocutores tienen cultura y disponibilidad necesaria para su comprensión y apreciación;

- Sólo con un guionamento personalizado es posible demostrar a los visitantes de la región la importancia de las rutas y circuitos para revelar la coherencia de las culturas, los valores de las culturas de los campos y de las sociedades, los asentamientos y el patrimonio natural y cultural, conseguir una más completa comprensión y disfrute de los hábitats, paisajes, patrimonio, tradiciones y costumbres, artes, historia y tradiciones, transformando los excursionistas en turistas.

- Desarrollar la preferencia del turista por las visitas y el consumo de productos turísticos diversos, partiendo de la experimentación indispensable, será uno de los medios más eficaces para transformar recursos en productos turísticos y los excursionistas en turistas, promoviendo un crecimiento muy fuerte en los ingresos ya que el turismo potenciará los comedores y el alojamiento y, probablemente, otras variantes de las Cadenas de Valor: tiendas y merchandising, entretenimiento, transporte y agencias de viaje. Por ello hemos concluido que es importante que la formación de guías turísticos logre instruirlos en las competencias prácticas y capacidad de investigación sobre los significados y orígenes del patrimonio, de los paisajes culturales "semisalvajes", una práctica que cualificará para el guionamento pero también proporcionará los conocimientos y maestrías para la creación de rutas y circuitos y el diseño de los guiones de visita.

¿Qué competencias deben tener los Guías Turísticos? Del perfil del Guía de Turismo Cultural al perfil de Guía de Turismo ambiental. Guías nacionales, regionales y locales de Turismo Ambiental

En este contexto y dada la dimensión interdisciplinaria y el sistema de equivalencias característicos de la educación superior, el acceso a la profesión de guía nacional puede estar basada no sólo en la frecuencia de una titulación en turismo, sino también en el reciclaje de titulaciones orientadas tradicionalmente a otras profesiones, sobre la base de extensión de la actividad de guionamento del patrimonio natural del patrimonio cultural.

Teniendo en cuenta los tres niveles de intervención territorial de los guías _ niveles local, regional y nacional, es aceptable menos requisitos de escolaridad y formación profesional para las áreas más restringidas, en particular el local, al menos durante un período, aunque largo, de adaptación e instalación de estas actividades profesionales. Pero cabe señalar en relación con el nivel de educación de los turistas que los guías acogen cada vez más visitantes con formación en la universidad ;

por lo que parece aceptable que los guías tengan también una educación académica del nivel superior, excepto en el caso del patrimonio local, en las zonas rurales en particular (por ejemplo, guías de caminantes, de aldeas, de granjas o bodegas) o de las actividades artesanas, es importante para la los turistas escuchar las personas que representan esa cultura artesana y tradicional, tales como recorridos por las rutas del vino, visitas a los talleres de artesanía, participación en el cultivo de los campos...

Contexto ideológico e pedagógico de la formación de los guías

La experiencia personal y empírica, pero evaluada con métodos científicos durante 30 años, las actividades de Guía en el yacimiento de Conimbriga _ Portugal, (ruinas de una ciudad romana, con Museo Monográfico y el paisaje del *oppidum* pobladas de villas), con una audiencia nacional e internacional, representativa de todas las clases sociales y niveles de edad, ha conducido a asociar esta actividad de guionamento al teatro, mientras recurso de reconstitución de la ciudad, de sus característica políticas, económicas y sociales de sus habitantes, del imaginario de costumbres, mitos y expresiones artísticas; una guía también tiene algunas semejanzas con la función de los actores.

Más allá del Teatro, también se asoció a las necesidades de formación y comunicación de los Guías la que fue una de las principales disciplinas de las escuelas clásicas, la Retórica. Según el diccionario, del latín *rhetorica*, originado en el griego *rhêtorikê*, literalmente, el arte/técnica de bien hablar. El sustantivo *rhêtôr*, "orador", significa el arte de utilizar la lengua para comunicarse de manera efectiva y persuasiva. También era conocido como un "arte dedicada a resolver discursivamente un asunto que requiere una decisión mediante el uso de estrategias de persuasión deliberadas dirigidas a un conjunto determinado de personas, con el objetivo de transformar un situación (y problemas) gracias a la adopción de nuevas formas de pensamiento y acción". Pero hay técnicas de comunicación modernas, ya sea oral, o escrita, utilizadas en la formación de locutores y presentadores que pueden dar contribuciones más importantes que la retórica para la formación de los Guías.

Intentamos procurar afinidades de la formación de los guías turística con la enseñanza superior de periodismo y comunicación social, en particular del periodismo de investigación, incluso por aspectos ideológicos y éticos que deben estar asociados con esta función y la respectiva formación. Hay en los medios de comunicación y en el periodismo métodos de investigación que son esenciales en la carrera de los guías de turismo, como la investigación de la información, el estudio de temas relacionados con la actividad en su contexto, para concluir en el aprendizaje de la escritura periodista y de la locución, dirigidas a un público más o menos determinado.

En los tres casos (Teatro, Retórica y Comunicación) creemos que las podemos considerar, en el contexto de la actividad de guía turístico, como las artes escénicas, en que el desempeño profesional en la escritura y en el discurso público es decisivo.

Obviamente esta visión debe ser transportada al currículo formativo, donde consideramos tres tipos de formación donde el componente práctico, experimental, es muy importante.

Vamos analizar estas tres opciones de paradigmas formativos de los guías y veremos si el lector crítico también entiendo que si ninguna es perfectamente compatible los con objetivos y contextos de la formación de guías turísticos, también su análisis detallada, incluyendo la bibliografía respectiva, lleva importantes contribuciones para el diseño de la estructura, disciplinas, metodologías o pedagogías apropiadas a la formación de distintos niveles y especialidades de guías turísticas.

Finalmente entendemos lícito añadir que estas tres funciones performativas podrían integrarse no sólo en una estructura curricular horizontal _ cursos de varios niveles hasta el topo de la titulación, y al mismo tiempo seguir un posgrado de estructura vertical de los 2 º y 3 º ciclos de la educación superior _ cursos de especialización, master, doctorado y post doctorado _ destinados a las artes escénicas y de la comunicación. Adelante al desarrollo curricular.

Contexto Teatral

Hay, como hemos intentado demostrar, grandes afinidades entre la planificación (escenificación /realización) y desempeño de la actividad teatral y la planificación y actividad (performance) del guía turístico.

Pero también hay grandes diferencias. En el teatro es un grupo de artistas que contra-actúan de forma prevista y articulada para poner en escena una dramaturgia, cuya representación es el objetivo del espectáculo, aunque los defensores del teatro como verdad (de la vida?) entiendan lo que es verdaderamente importante es el actor, la suya performance, su verdad y el público, cuando hay teatro real, contra-actúa, al menos emocionalmente, quizá filosóficamente, con el actor, este siendo también un intermediario entre el dramaturgo, el director escénico y el público.

Escenarios, sonido y luz son medios auxiliares del poner en escena, con distintas importancias al largo de la historia del teatro. Pero, deben considerarse como una oportunidad para ayudar a la tarea del guía. Texto y imágenes que se presentan en los circuitos y rutas turísticas son idénticos sistemas auxiliares idénticos a los escenarios del teatro. Incluso en los senderos al aire libre los guías utilizan con éxito imágenes impresas o en formato digital. Música luz y sonidos, son auxiliares del guía, en particular en contextos museológicos. En el paisaje, especialmente en el campo y el mar, hay olores, cantos y voces de los entes y cosas naturales_ melodías del viento, de las aguas corrientes o agitadas, las tormentas en el cielo, paletas de colores, sonidos de rebaños, canto de los pájaros y las voces de los animales salvajes... materias que el guía tradicional aún no conoce, reduciendo su función a ver, leer, interpretan.

Aunque la preparación de la dramaturgia y de la performance pueda parecer más importante y requerir más tiempo en el teatro que en la guionamento, toda esa planificación debe ser llevada a cabo también para el ejercicio cualificado del guionamento, sobre todo cuando se pretende una actividad profesional con alta calidad de contexto y forma, así como para lograr la vinculación emocional e intelectual de los turistas.

Pero en el guionamento, como regla general, sólo existe un actor. Podemos objetar que en el teatro también se representar monólogos. Pero hay algo en guionamento, que al contrario del teatro, es más importante que el actor: el patrimonio que el guía va a presentar, de la mejor manera posible. Es, de hecho, el objetivo principal del guionamento. Este patrimonio es tan importante que, en una comparación con el teatro, podemos considerarlo equiparado a la "dramaturgia" de la obra teatral. Pero el actor no puede tomar el protagonismo en detrimento del patrimonio. El papel de la guía no es se valorar a si mismo como un actor, quién debe estar en el centro de atención en el escenario es el patrimonio y su componentes materiales y inmateriales. El papel de la guía es exactamente de valorar el patrimonio, sus componentes, sus cualidades, su historia y en la medida que mejor sea su desempeño más saldrá valorado de la "escena".

Es posible evaluar este desempeño "midiendo" la apreciación del público con respecto a dos aspectos: el valor que se asignó después del guionamento al patrimonio y la puntuación que el público concede a la performance del guía turístico, más allá de buena o mala, siguiendo una red de evaluación cuantitativa y cualitativa.

Para completar esta evaluación sintética: la contribución de las pedagogías y metodologías del teatro, de la escenificación y de los respectivos medios auxiliares, para la preparación y aplicación de las actividades de guionamento será tanto más significativa cuando más exigente fuer la exigencia de calidad en cada guionamento.

Esta lógica se aplica a la determinación de la importancia de los componentes del teatro en la planificación y pedagogía de la formación profesional de los guías.

Examinemos el caso particular de la escenografía en los contextos de guionamento y de la museología.

Escenografía en el teatro o en el cinema ayuda a la representación y es esencial para la vivencia, para la dramatización de la escena. Llevando esta idea para el guionamento turístico, postulamos la necesidad dl guía de turismo ambiental recurrir a aspectos que ayuden a presente/interpretar el patrimonio, a lograr una mejor comprensión y vivencia de su información oral, como por ejemplo: mapas que ayuden a localizar, plantas, alzados y secciones, imágenes, dibujos, esquemas, as veces acompañados de textos cortos. Estos medios auxiliares que tanto pueden ser transportadas por la guía si son fácilmente transportables, como existieren en el lugar a visitar (museo, jardín botánico, paisaje, etc.) que el guía puede usar.

Cuando hay guionamento el más importante son las fotos, dibujos y diagramas que ayudan al guía. L' información existente sobre el patrimonio puede ayudar el trabajo del guía, condicionar o dificultar a visita. Los museólogos, por esta razón, deberían escuchar los guías en estos aspectos. El desempeño de las funciones de guía es eficaz en el análisis de la oportunidad y calidad de la información existente en el material editado o en los carteles.

La existencia de música apropiada, presentada y seleccionada con gusto, puede ser apropiada en las pausas de la visita o como contexto musical de fondo, para ayudar a crear o recordar un ambiente. La luz también es muy importante. En la presentación de grabados rupestres al aire libre, por ejemplo, el ángulo del sol es la clave para revelar los dibujos escritos. Ya en las cuevas y dentro de los museos la iluminación es una técnica esencial a la revelación, respetuosa, de la arte.

Evolucionando en este discurso, entramos en la museología y dejamos de hablar solamente de guionamento. Cuando se trata de promover una comprensión más profunda de la información de temas científicos por la revelación de aspectos más detallados a los visitantes que no son especialistas, entramos también en el campo de los Centros de Interpretación, que cuando orientados para el auto guionamento, la exploración orientada individual o en grupo pequeños, la información disponible construida como proceso de investigación, teóricamente dispensa el guionamento. Pero no dispensa la presencia de alguien del personal para dar una u otra explicación deseada, ayudar ante las dificultades de los visitantes, animar personas más perezosas, ejemplificando lo que es "el premio" de la exploración de los módulos y equipamientos del centro de interpretación.

Si nos fijamos en el centro de interpretación como un escenario que casi llega a representar la obra de teatro por sí mismo, puesto que el visitante busque y haga su selección entre varias alternativas, tenderemos a non valorar la necesidad de guionamento. Todavía, especialmente en el caso del analfabetismo electrónico, concluiremos que es necesaria la actividad de un actor para simplificar y ayudar al visitante a explorar los equipamientos de la museografía, sin lo cual, solos, no serán capaces de lo hacer. Antes los visitantes que no demuestran suficiente capacidad o motivación, es imprescindible la presencia de este alentador con conocimiento de la materia y del sistema, dotado de capacidad pedagógica.

Muchos aspectos del patrimonio cultural necesitan urgentemente ser revelados con medios eficaces para atingir a sus públicos específicos. Según lo indicado por Manuel de Lacerda

> "Comunicar el patrimonio cultural implica conocer, cada momento y en cada contexto, lo que queremos comunicar y a quién, seleccionando los medios y sobre todo, saber la razón por qué lo hacemos."
> (Lacerda, 2015:3)

En la actualidad, esto se aplica a todo lo que tenga injerencia con el desarrollo sostenible, la conservación y rehabilitación del patrimonio, recursos naturales y biodiversidad, patrimonio cultural y patrimonio natural.

La Retórica

El paralelismo con la retórica es menos importante, porque actualmente hay una devaluación general del arte de la oratoria, confundida con falaces discursos de los políticos y la pompa de la oratoria tradicional. El guía moderno no debe usar estilos, manías y silogismos de oratoria, pero un lenguaje claro y accesible, tan fluido y honesto como sea posible.

Sin embargo algunos métodos de oratoria no deben ser desperdiciados, aunque no directamente aplicables, sino como aspectos, modos de ver, que pueden ayudar a calificar la enseñanza de los guías. Éstos también deben tener un lenguaje correcto, fluido y comprensible.

La retórica apela a la audiencia en tres frentes: logos, pathos y ethos. La preparación del discurso y su exposición requieren atención a cinco dimensiones que se complementan entre sí (los cinco cánones o momentos de retórica): la invención, la selción de los contenidos del discurso; diseño, organización de los contenido en un todo estructurado; elocución, expresión adecuada de los contenidos; memoria, la memorización del discurso y la declamación del discurso, en que la modulación de la voz y los gestos deben estar en línea con el contenido (esto 5 momento no siempre se considera).

Pero se entiende que quizás la mayor contribución de la retórica para el guionamento es o puede ser la enseñanza que cualquier "intervención" debería ser preparada, aunque en guionamento no debe ser leída y en vez de enfática, pomposa, sino ser natural y convincente. El guía debe mostrar cultura, capacidad de comunicación, entusiasmo por el patrimonio que presenta para lo valorar.

Comunicación Social

Los medios de comunicación social, como anteriormente postulamos, integran actividades que también son esenciales en la carrera de los de la guías de turismo, como la búsqueda de información, el estudio o investigación de temas relacionados con la actividad, para completar en el aprendizaje de la redacción periodística y de la locución.

En muchos aspectos este tipo de formación está pensado para sustituir la retórica, porque el "lenguaje" de los medios de comunicación, adaptados a los conceptos y costumbres actuales, sustituye la retórica.

Perfil de los guías turísticos

Pensando en las expectativas de aquellos que buscan el turismo cultural y el turismo de naturaleza, así como el turismo en los espacios rurales y en lo que será un bueno circuito y un bueno guionamento realizado por un guía turístico especializado, creemos que ambos (circuito y guionamento) deben valorar y vivenciar el patrimonio.

Pero hay que tener en cuenta entre lo que el público espera del Guía en contextos culturales diferentes. La distinción principal será entre el guía que actúa dentro de puertas (museos y palacios), que se espera sea más especializado, y lo que hace el guiado al aire libre sea en paisaje urbano o natural, que se espera tenga una relación más amplia con el patrimonio que presenta.

Pensando también en lo que es una estrategia de desarrollo de turismo sostenible, estaremos en una posición para ser capaces de proponer un perfil profesional adecuado para el guía turístico.

Hay tres ejes fundamentales para la definición de este perfil:

- el conocimiento científico y cultural, multidisciplinario y transdisciplinario;

- el conocimiento y el arte de comunicar;

- y el entendimiento de lo que es el fenómeno turístico, su importancia a la cultura, la sociedad y la economía y los principales aspectos relacionados con la sostenibilidad de la actividad y a la conservación del patrimonio.

Pesquisando el origen de los conceptos, volvemos a Atenas y al siglo de Pericles, para asistir al nacimiento de la designación de pedagogo que era el esclavo que acompañaba y guardaba los niños y jóvenes cuando iban a la escuela. Después de reflexionar que estos maestros no podían utilizar cualquier medio punitivo, todavía eran totalmente responsables por las escoltar en paz y seguridad, la imagen del guía de turismo emergió como una aparición Al igual que sucede con el guía, que no es un esclavo, pero abrumados ante la regla comercial que "el cliente siempre tiene razón", quiere ese esclavo, quiere el guía, tienen que ser investidos de una autoridad reconocida, gracias a la calidad de su postura, su conocimiento y su desempeño. ¿Por consiguiente, cuestionamos si las astucias inventadas por estos esclavos cultos, no estuvieran en el origen de las ciencias de la educación? Y entendemos por qué tal título (pedagogo) fue dado a los esclavos cultos griegos que educaban a la nobleza romana.

Estamos convictos que los conocimientos científicos y técnicos y maestrías, incluyendo las competencias en comunicación propuestos en este perfil de guía turístico (aquí nos referimos especialmente a las guías nacionales y regionales) crean una tal exigencia que dudamos pueda ser satisfecha totalmente adquiriendo una titulación normal de 3 años prevista en el Acuerdo de Boloña. En lo itinerario formativo que proponemos, el guía debe buscar la formación científica de base en una titulación de la universidad (o escuela técnica superior) reorganizada o reciclada para la iniciación en el nuevo paradigma del turismo ambiental y en los problemas de comunicación en el turismo.

Como conocimiento científico de base para la interpretación de los paisajes humanizados y semisalvajes, definidos como paisajes culturales, la formación puede seguir distintas opciones dependiendo del tipo de recursos turísticos de su mercado concreto de trabajo, de la biología, geología, geografía, ingeniería agrícola...a la arquitectura del paisaje. Todas estas titulaciones incluyen el conocimiento de varias ciencias necesarias para la interpretación de estos tipos de paisajes.

Los aspectos antes mencionados de los conocimientos y competencias específicas relacionadas con las funciones de guía turístico también serían objeto de cursos de posgrado.

Parece claro que las características personales y conocimientos en materia de comunicación, y los conocimientos científico necesarios, no serán exactamente los mismos para diferentes tipos de patrimonio, es decir, para quien guía en la naturaleza, o que guía en uno museo de arte o que guía en un museo de ciencias, Pero no parece factible promover cursos a nivel universitario para la formación en cada tipo de guionamento. De hecho ni una certificación sólo destinada a guías de turismo será capaz de responder a todas las necesidades de formación. Por lo tanto la necesidad de formación continuada y de nivel superior.

Sin embargo es obvio que en cada contexto del patrimonio y cada contexto museológico, habrá lugar para una formación específica de menor duración o incluso cursos de postgrado, con investigación y producción de tesis.

Todo lo que se dice nos conducirá a un perfil más amplio de competencias y funciones del guía de turismo ambiental. Esto significa que el guía de lo presente y del futuro, debe tener su plan de estudios curricular, no sólo de los componentes de la lectura y interpretación del patrimonio, sino también para rehabilitar, conservar y gestionar. Esto significa probablemente que desarrollará tres tipos de trabajo determinados por las fluctuaciones de la demanda y estacionalidad: guiar, gestionar los patrimonios de forma sostenible y crear pequeñas empresas (un restaurante, un pequeño alojamiento). Estos temas importantes, por razones obvias, no se pueden desarrollar en el ámbito de este artículo.

3. Conclusiones

La comunicación turística exige construir un discurso específico, adaptado a distintos públicos, que no puede ser confundido con la transcripción de textos eruditos para los estratos sociales superiores o con la banalización de la información para las capas populares.

Ese discurso tiene exigencias éticas y morales que deben orientar el trabajo técnico y la formación científica, y que pueden ser estudiados con base en el concepto de "gusto", concepto de la filosofía que contiene una dimensión estética y moral, en el marco del cambio de paradigma del turismo con la ascensión del Turismo Ambiental_ Turismo Cultural, Turismo de naturaleza y Turismo en Espacio Rural.

La comunicación en turismo puede beneficiar de las nuevas tecnologías, todavía el guía es indispensable para promover la lectura, interpretación y desfrute del paisaje cultural, que es un proceso complexo, personal y dialectico, lo cual necesita de un previo conocimiento del patrimonio tangible (material) y intangible (inmaterial).

En tesis podemos concluir que la comunicación clara, completa y perfecta depende más de atributos ideológicos y morales (éticos) do que del simple conocimiento científico y técnico, sin embargo que el teatro, la retórica y los medios de comunicación constituyen fuentes de formación de los guías poco

La filosofía que determina el nuevo gusto de la clase media es la filosofía ambiental. Y la ética que determina las reglas morales del turismo moderno y de la deontología profesional es la ética ambiental, fundada con base en la crítica del antropocentrismo y del etnocentrismo.

4. Referencias Bibliográficas

Libros

Cabral, F. C., (1956). Fundamentos da Arquitectura Paisagista. Lisboa: Instituto de Conservação da Natureza.

Galopim de Carvalho, A. M., Queirós, A. (1999). Geomonumentos. Editora Liga de Amigos de Conimbriga, Museu Monográfico de Conimbriga.

Kuhn, T.S. (1962). The Structure of Scientific Revolutions. Chicago: University of Chicago Press.

Morales, J.; Guerra, F. J.; Serantes, A. (2009) Bases para la Definición de Competencias en Interpretación del Patrimonio - Fundamentos teóricos y metodológicos para definir las Competencias Profesionales de Especialistas en Interpretación del Patrimonio en España. Seminario Permanente de Interpretación del Patrimonio, Centro Nacional de Educación Ambiental - CENEAM, España.

Queirós, A., (2009). Programa de Investigação sobre Turismo Cultural e de Natureza e desenvolvimento sustentável. Relatório Final. Departamento de Economia, Gestão e Engenharia Industrial (DEGEI). Universidade de Aveiro ("Research program on Cultural Tourism and Tourism of Nature and Sustainable Development." Post-doctoral Research. University of Aveiro)

Swarbrooke (2002). Sustainable Tourism Management, New York: CABI Publishing.

Ward, B., Dubos, R (1972). Nous n'avons qu'une terre. Trad.fr. Paris: Editions Denoël.

Ziffer, K.A. (1989). Ecotourism: The Uneasy Alliance. Washington DC: Conservation International.

Artículos de revistas

Lacerda, M. (2015). Revista nº 3 de la Dirección General de Patrimonio Cultural, Portugal (p.6)

Larrère, C. (2006). Éthiques de l'environnement. Revue Multitudes, nº 24. (Ethics of the environnement) Edition virtuelle. Internet Sources, accessed in 03.02.2015

Queirós, A (2015). Cultural tourism on a changing paradigm. International Journal of Scientific Management and Tourism. iManagement and Tourism. Córdoba, Spain, (pp. 179-216)

Queirós, A (2015). Cultural tourism and the new economy of heritage. International Journal of Scientific Management and Tourism. iManagement and Tourism. Vol. 1-2. Córdoba, Spain, (pp. 229-251)

Queirós, A (2017). Tourism Management of human heritage on a changing paradigm of Environment Tourism. International Journal of Scientific Management and Tourism. iManagement and Tourism. Vol. 3-4. Córdoba, Spain, (pp.37-59)

Capítulos de libros

Berleant, A. (2011). Changing Landscapes, Keynote lecture at "Transition Landscapes/ Paysages en Transition," International Conference, Lisbon, Portugal

Fennell, D. (2011). Ethics and Tourism. Philosophical Issues in Tourism, Edited by John Tribe. Bristol: Channel View Publications, pp. 211-226.

Queirós, A. (2012). Landscape tourism. Manual of philosophy and Landscape Architecture. A handbook. Coordination of Adriana Veríssimo Serrão. Edition CFUL, pp. 177-187.

Queirós, A. (2013). Cultural agents of change and the sunset of environmental services. And Old farming mountain systems. The economy and ecology of heathlands. Published by Alterra (Wageningen-UR (University and Research Centre). INBO (Belgium) KNNV Publishing. Nederland, pp. 49-50 and pp. 31-48.

Eisenstein, S. (2002). O sentido do filme. Edit Zahar. S. Paulo, Brasil

Data and internet sources

[TIES] (2011). Recuperado de Ecotourism. Principles of Ecotourism, The International Ecotourism Society, [http://www.ecotourism.org/what-is-ecotourism] Internet Sources, accessed in 03.02.2015

WTO (2001). Global Code of Ethics for Tourism. Recuperado de [http://www.unwto.org/ethics/full_text/en/pdf/Codigo_Etico_Ing.pdf] .Internet Sources, accessed in 03.02.2015

UNCHE (1972). Action Plan for the Human Environment. B.5. Development and Environment. Recuperado de United Nations Conference on the Human Environment A/CONF.48/14/Rev.1 - June 1972 Stockholm, Sweden.

EDUCACIÓN SOBRE LOS DERECHOS DEL ANIMAL EN LA SERIE DE ANIMACIÓN ESPAÑOLA MOFLI, EL ÚLTIMO KOALA (1987).

Oliver Salas Herrera
Doctorando en Comunicación en la Universidad de Cádiz, España.

Resumen

Introducción. El presente estudio de caso versa sobre la representación de los derechos del animal en la serie de animación española *Mofli, el último koala* (Jordi Amorós, 1987), producida y estrenada por Televisión Española en 1987 en co-producción con Equip Studio de Animación. El objetivo de esta retrospectiva es determinar cuál fue la filosofía inculcada en esta materia a los espectadores y espectadoras –asunto relevante si tenemos en cuenta que el público infantil de entonces son los adultos del presente–. **Metodología-desarrollo.** Para ello hemos aplicado la metodología cualitativa a todos los episodios de la misma siguiendo dos pautas. En primer lugar se ha elaborado el esquema actancial (Greimas, 1966) de la producción para analizar el discurso narrativo y, posteriormente, se ha comparado el relato de la ficción con los catorce artículos de la Declaración Universal de los Derechos del Animal (1977). **Resultados.** La historia de Mofli invita desde la propia función de los actantes del relato a sensibilizarnos en la importancia de la protección hacia los animales. **Conclusiones.** La trama prioriza la cuestión de la extinción de las especies sin dejar a un lado otras temáticas presentes en la Declaración Universal de los Derechos del Animal (1997) como la importancia del cuidado de la naturaleza, el rechazo al abandono o la explotación animal.

Palabras claves

Derechos de los animales, ecología, discurso, televisión, dibujos.

1. Introducción: La importancia de la retrospectiva

El presente estudio de caso versa sobre la ficción de animación española *Mofli, el último koala* (Jordi Amorós, 1987) siendo el objetivo determinar cuál fue la filosofía inculcada en materia de derechos del animal a los espectadores y espectadoras de esta serie producida y estrenada por Televisión Española en 1987 en co-producción con Equip Studio de Animación.

> [...] *Mofli, el último koala* constituyó una de las series más populares de los años 80 que transmitían un mensaje ecologista necesario para entender que había animales en peligro de extinción. (Yébenes Cortés, Mesonero Izquierdo, Rodríguez Díaz, Viñolo Locubiche, 2016: 92)

Para quienes no conozcan esta producción se trata de una serie de animación española 2D que aborda la extinción de las especies en una distopía ambientada en el siglo XXI. En ella, la sociedad globalizada ha priorizado un consumismo tecnológico sin tener en cuenta la conservación del medio ambiente y, como consecuencia, se ha descuidado la vida animal provocando una extensa lista de especies desaparecidas. Los koalas formaban parte de dicho listado hasta que un investigador llamado Doctor Fool informa a los medios de comunicación de haber avistado a Mofli en el bosque de Rivermint. La noticia crea tal revuelo a nivel mundial que varios personajes de distintas nacionalidades viajan hasta Australia para capturar al último koala. Será Corina, una pre-adolescente sin mayor ambición que proteger al tierno animal, quien se encargará junto a sus aliados de evitar que los forasteros rapten al pequeño Mofli.

En esta investigación sobre la televisión pública española planteamos la retrospectiva audiovisual como un modo necesario de conocimiento que nos puede ayudar a discernir cuáles fueron los mensajes promovidos y/o aceptados socialmente en el ayer para comprender nuestro presente; siendo esta mirada al ayer una herramienta idónea para analizar la Teoría de Cultivo de la etapa que nos ocupa:

> [...] se refiere a aquellos efectos producidos como consecuencia de una exposición acumulativa, durante largos lapsos de tiempo, a un sistema de mensajes estable y repetitivo en sus contenidos (Morgan y Signorielli, 1990 citado en Jiménez Sánchez, 2015: 142)

2. Antecedentes: Animación y educación ambiental

Calvo y Gutiérrez (2007) describen la educación ambiental (EA) como una corriente de pensamiento que surgió tras la Segunda Guerra Mundial. (p. 21).

Según ambos autores, la primera referencia a este concepto se publicó a finales de los sesenta por parte del norteamericano William STAPP y su equipo de la Universidad de Michigan en el primer número del *Journal of Environmental Education*:

> La educación ambiental tiene como objetivo producir unos ciudadanos dotados de conocimientos sobre el entorno biofísico y sus problemas, conscientes de cómo resolver eso problemas, y motivados para trabajar en busca de una solución (1969) (íbidem: 23)

No obstante, aunque el concepto apareciese de forma tardía, la ecología y la empatía hacia los animales ya eran temas educativos recurrentes ligados a la animación desde sus orígenes. Si bien el cine de imagen real no se permitió dar excesivo protagonismo a los animales debido a la dificultad que suponía rodar con ellos, el cine animado sí lo haría gracias al abanico de posibilidades creativas que ofrecía el lápiz.

Ya en los comienzos de los dibujos animados muchos animales se convirtieron en personajes carismáticos aún reconocibles a día de hoy. Tal es el caso, entre otros muchos ejemplos, del gato Félix (1919), el ratón Mickey Mouse (1928) o los múltiples y alocados animales de los Looney Tunes como el cerdito Porky (1935) o el Pato Lucas (Daffy Duck, 1937). Aunque unos protagonistas eran más antropomorfos que otros, los distintos estilos lograban empatizar con el público pues daban a conocer sus propios conflictos de forma clara y divertida.

En principio, muchas de estas historias eran sencillos *sketches* cuya temática principal abordaba las luchas instintivas y estereotipadas entre determinadas especies como ejemplifica la relación entre Tom y Jerry (1940); pero lo que comenzó con el clásico humor de golpes y tortazos disparatados, fue evolucionando y tornándose más complejo. En *All Wet* (Walt Disney, 1927), cortometraje del conejo Oswald (1927), ya se planteaba cómicamente el dilema de la alimentación carnívora a través del perro que llora al simpatizar con la expresiva salchicha del perrito caliente que pensaba comerse; para poco después en *Fresh here* (Friz Freleng, 1942) presenciamos la conflictiva relación entre el humano cazador y el animal salvaje. En esta primera aparición del parlante Bugs Bunny (1940), el conejo defiende con firmeza sus derechos a la vez que aparta de su pecho el arma del cazador –discurso llamativo si tenemos en cuenta que esta obra audiovisual es anterior a la propia redacción de la *Declaración Universal de los Derechos del Animal* (1977)–. Por otro lado, producciones como *Ferdinand the Bull* (Dick Rickard, 1938) de Walt Disney serían más concretas en cuanto a su temática, abordando en este caso el aún polémico debate sobre la tauromaquia. Pese a recibir el Oscar a Mejor Cortometraje de Animación en 1939, esta adaptación del cuento del escritor Munro Leaf y el ilustrador Robert Lawson fue censurada en España durante la dictadura franquista.

Con los años, a estos y otros formatos de corta duración, se sumó la aparición del cine animado. En él se ofrecía la posibilidad de investigar nuevos horizontes creativos al poder contar historias más dilatadas donde los personajes pudiesen desarrollarse más cómodamente. Al igual que el cine de imagen real se exploró con mayor profundidad el drama, logrando alcanzar mayor protagonismo que en etapas anteriores. Desde el propio guion se enfatizó la emotividad de las historias y surgieron nuevas sendas para comunicar las moralejas. En este sentido, la educación ambiental y los dibujos parecían darse la mano con mayor firmeza pues si ya en los orígenes la naturaleza y los animales eran las estrellas carismáticas, ¿por qué el recién nacido cine animado no profundizarían en la misma dirección?

Dado el contexto y tras el éxito de *Blancanieves y los siete enanitos* (Snow White and the Seven Dwarfs, David Hand, 1937) no tardarían en llegar otros proyectos más centrados en la empatía hacia los animales como *Bambi* (David Hand, 1942) o la adaptación de la novela de Dodie Smith titulada *101 Dálmatas* (One Hundred and One Dalmatians, Clyde Geronimi, Wolfgang Reitherman, Hamilton Luske, 1961) donde se invita al rechazo del uso de pieles en la vestimenta que representa la villana Cruella de Vil.

Al igual que de forma generalista parecía ocurrir en con las películas animadas, la ecología y la presencia animal se convirtieron en requisitos estereotipados presentes en las series televisadas destinadas al público infantil –también en las producciones japonesas de *anime*–. En España fue *Heidi, la niña de los Alpes* (Arupusu no Shōjo Haiji, Isao Takahata, 1974) la serie de estructura lineal que marcó un antes y un después en 1975. Su trama abarca desde la sostenibilidad de la vida tradicional; el rechazo al maltrato animal y al biocidio cuando quieren sacrificar a Copo de Nieve por no poder dar leche (Capítulo 14); o la exaltación sobre lo saludable de la vida junto a la naturaleza representada tanto en la enfermedad de Heidi al estar en Fráncfort (Capítulo 32) o en la propia recuperación de Clara cuando les visita a la casa del abuelo (Capítulo 50).

A consecuencia del éxito de la adaptación de Johanna Spyri llegaron otros títulos de filosofía similar como *El bosque de Tallac* (Seton Dôbut-suki Kuma no ko Jakkī, Fumio Kurokawa, Masao Kuroda, Yoshihiro Kuroda, 1977) o *Banner y Flapy* (Seton Dôbutsuki Risu no bannâ, Yos-hihiro Kuroda, 1979) –ambos distribuidos por BRB Internacional antes de comenzar su trayectoria como productora nacional–. Una caracte-rística común de estas series es que logran otorgar un gran protago-nismo a la naturaleza sin necesidad de darles vida propia como ocurría en *Árboles y flores* (Flowers and trees, Burt Gillett, 1932) sino proyec-tando un marco utópico y liberador asociado a la felicidad, donde la im-portancia de la calidad de los escenarios pintados a mano son difícil-mente reproducibles actualmente para televisión.

Este noviazgo duradero entre la animación y la educación ambiental in-fluenció también en la producción de series nacionales. La más afamada internacionalmente es *David el gnomo* (Luis Ballester, 1985) de BRB In-ternacional; donde los vegetarianos gnomos educan con firmeza contra la contaminación o la caza furtiva. Esta productora y distribuidora se convirtió en la más prolífica y exitosa de España allanando el terreno a otras series que, como *Mofli, el último koala* (Jordi Amorós, 1987), traba-jarían en coproducción con TVE durante la década de los ochenta.

Figura 1: Bosque de Rivermint. (González y Amorós, 1987: Capítulo 3)

3. Mofli: una producción controvertida

En sus orígenes, la serie producida por TVE y la catalana Equip Studio de Animación se ideó como una producción de 26 episodios –estándar generalizado en las producciones de dibujos animados de Televisión Española en los ochenta–. Por el contrario, debido a problemas durante la producción, la serie se redujo a la mitad tanto en capítulos como en presupuesto:

> El contrato entre TVE y la productora, Equip Studio Animación, SA, comienza a elaborarse el 17 de septiembre de 1984, a partir de la idea y proyecto que presenta Jaime González, y se formaliza el 13 de febrero de 1985. El primer proyecto consta de 26 capítulos de una duración comercial de media hora, por cuyos derechos de explotación TVE se compromete a pagar 130 millones de pesetas. [...] Sin embargo, el 24 de julio de 1986 se formaliza un nuevo contrato, "por expirar el plazo de entrega contemplado en el anterior", y se reduce en un 50% el número de episodios. "El precio que TVE, SA, pagará por estos 13 capítulos", se escribe, "será de 65 millones de pesetas, de los cuales 61.360.000 pesetas se reconoce haber anticipado". (Pérez, 1987)

Como consecuencia de los titulares publicados, consultamos a Amorós sobre estas publicaciones y quiso matizar aquellos acontecimientos:

> Era período navideño y, Laboratorios Riera, donde procesaban el material, cerro unos días por vacaciones. Los episodios que había que entregar a TVE según contrato no habían terminado de etalonarse –una corrección del laboratorio para unificar el color–. Puestos en contacto con TVE se les notificó este pequeño retraso –unos pocos días–. Su respuesta fue tajante: o entregábamos los episodios o "prescindían el contracto". No hubo opción y entregamos los episodios a "medio etalonar". Los periódicos de la época informaron "al mundo" con grandes titulares que Pilar Miró había "rechazado la serie por falta de calidad". Pasadas las navidades, se reanudo el etalonaje de la serie por los Laboratorios Riera y la serie fue aprobada por TVE. [...] (Amorós, 2018. Entrevista. Elaboración propia)

Otro conflicto acontecido durante el proceso de producción se produjo cuando TVE solicito la modificación del personaje de Bailosolo puesto que, según destaca Amorós, el diseño de Enrique Ventura llevaba varios episodios realizados.

Tras superar las adversidades, los trece capítulos de *Mofli, el último koala* (1987) se estrenaron en TVE-1 a las seis de la tarde el 30 de septiembre de 1987, concluyendo la emisión completa el 23 de diciembre del mismo año. Mofli gozó de una gran acogida y traspasó fronteras. Se exportó y dobló a países como Portugal, Chile, Francia y Ucrania; llegando a editarse en formato VHS tanto en España como en Argentina.

Posteriormente, volvió a emitirse en España en diversas ocasiones aunque no se ha vuelto a editar tras aquel formato VHS.

Consultamos a Jordi Amorós sobre el estado del *copión original* y según nos informa debería estar en posesión de la Filmoteca Catalana pues "ellos se quedaron con todos los negativos de los Laboratorios Riera cuando quebró". (ídem). Dependiendo de su estado podría editarse un futuro lanzamiento de la serie remasterizada en DVD.

4. Método – Desarrollo del trabajo

Para llevar a cabo este análisis se ha aplicando la metodología cualitativa y se ha estructurado el estudio siguiendo dos procedimientos principales:

- En primer lugar se ha abordado el discurso del relato realizando el esquema actancial de A. J. Greimas (1966). Concretamente tomamos la modificación propuesta por la teórica francesa Anne Ubersfeld, quien –como explica Norma Roman–, sitúa "al sujeto entre el destinador y el destinatario y al objeto entre el ayudante y el oponente, pues considera que el conflicto ocurre en torno al objeto" (Román, 2007: 57)

- En segundo lugar se ha contrastado el argumento de los trece capítulos de la ficción con los catorce artículos de la *Declaración Universal de los Derechos del Animal* (1977). En este apartado valoraremos si las escenas invitan o no al cumplimiento de los artículos representados y determinaremos el enfoque principal de la serie basándonos en los temas y subtemas más presentes, omitidos o con menor presencia en el relato.

4.1. Resultados del esquema actancial

Mofli, el último koala (1987) es una animación con *trama serial* –argumento continuo–, por lo que solo se requiere la elaboración de un esquema actancial general para exponer los distintos actantes del argumento completo.

> Eje *destinador-destinatario*: "Es el del control de los valores y, por tanto, de la ideología" [...] Eje *sujeto-objeto*: "Traza la trayectoria del héroe y la búsqueda del héroe o del protagonista [...]. Es el eje del querer". [...] Eje *adyuvante-oponente*: "Produce las circunstancias y las modalidades de la acción y no es necesariamente representado por personajes". (Pavis, 1998: 29)

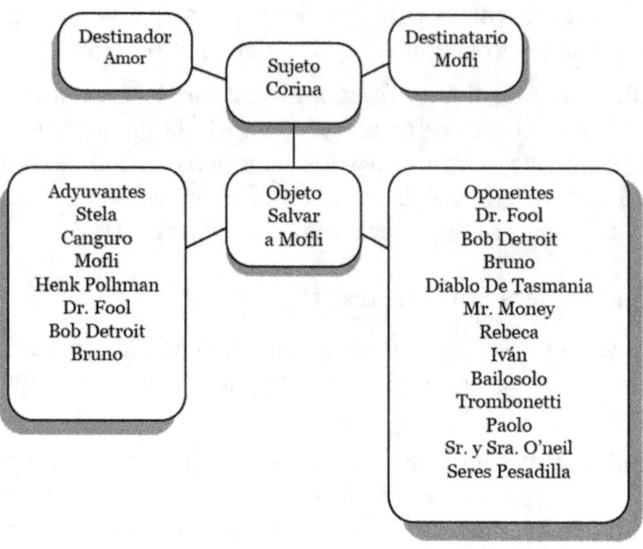

Figura 2: Esquema Actancial de *Mofli, el último koala (1987)*. Elaboración propia (2018).

Corina (*Sujeto*) desea salvar (*Objeto*) a Mofli (*Destinatario*). En la serie el *Destinador* es el amor protector que siente la chica (*Sujeto*) hacia el koala (*Destinatario*). Así, mientras que los *Adyuvantes* ayudarán al *Sujeto* a que cumpla su deseo, los *Oponentes* se interpondrán directa o indirectamente en el *Objeto* de la pequeña (*Sujeto*).

Figura 3: Corina piensa en Mofli. (González y Amorós, 1987: Capítulo 3)

Si bien los actantes del *Destinador* (amor hacia los animales), *Sujeto* (Corina) y *Destinatario* (Mofli) conservan su rol durante toda la historia, el eje *adyuvante-oponente* requiere un desglose más detallado ya que cada personaje tiene unas motivaciones propias para ejercer su rol. Primero desglosamos aquellos que poseen un rol fijo (grupo 1 y 2) y luego a los actantes que cambian de posicionamiento durante la trama (grupo 3):

1. *Adyuvantes*:
- Henk Polhman: Su motivación es el amor hacia Corina, por ello le pide que lleve a Mofli a casa para evitar que lo capturen (Capítulo 8).

- Stela: Es una mariposa. Su motivación es la amistad hacia Corina. Stela salva a Mofli de Iván (Capítulo 6) y de Paolo (Capítulo 10).

- El Canguro Enano: Actúa por solidaridad. Salva a Mofli al enseñarle a saltar a dos patas y poder así desplazarse tras haber sido herido durante el ataque del diablo de tasmania (Capítulo 11).

- Mofli: Además de *Destinatario* es *Adyuvante* de Corina puesto actúa por supervivencia y obedece las pautas de Corina al salvarse a sí mismo del diablo de tasmania (Capítulo 7 y 11).

- Los Cocodrilos: En este caso son ayudantes indirectos ya que, gracias a comerse la mochila de Bruno–, Mr. Money, Iván, Bailosolo y Rebeca creerán que estos han devorado a Mofli (Capítulo 13).

2. *Oponentes:*

- Mr. Money: Multimillonario coleccionista de especies disecadas. Decide ir en busca del koala para disecarlo y complacer a Rebeca al tener "el broche de oro para su colección" (Capítulo 3). Para ello ofrecerá un rescate por el koala (Capítulo 8).

- Rebeca: Comparte la misma motivación que su abuelo Mr. Money aunque su carácter es más incisivo y caprichoso. Esto se observa cuando ordena a Iván que consiga un koala incluso cuando se creen extintos (Capítulo 1). Rebeca es además es quien avisa a Iván, Bailosolo y Mr. Money de la presencia de Mofli en las Rocas Blancas aprovechando esta revelación inconsciente que hace el joven Bruno (Capítulo 13).

- Iván: Su motivación es cumplir su trabajo como cazador furtivo al servicio de Mr. Money –trabajo que realiza aparentemente más por placer que por dinero–. Este personaje es el que infunde más terror de todos los *Oponentes*.

Figura 4: Mr. Money, Iván y Rebeca en el Capítulo 3. (González y Amorós, 1987)

- Bailosolo: Es un estafador y un embaucador interesado. Su motivación es hacerse con la recompensa que ofrece Mr. Money por el koala (Capítulo 8).

- Trombonetti: Su motivación es económica. Tras oír la noticia en televisión decide viajar a Australia para capturar al koala y exhibirlo en su circo (Capítulo 2).

- Paolo: Paolo es el ayudante de Trombonetti. Comparte objetivos. Será él quien tras un accidente en globo descubra a Mofli e intente capturarlo (Capítulo 10).

- Señor O'neill y Señora O'neill: Sus acciones como Oponentes son conjuntas. No realizan actos directos contra el Objeto de Corina pero su motivación es atraer clientes a Rirvermint sin importar si el turismo masificado afecta al hábitat de Mofli (Capítulo 3). Piensan que el koala no existe pero fingen creer la historia por los beneficios que pueda generar la nueva popularidad de Rivermint.

- El Diablo de Tasmania: Ataca a Mofli como depredador en dos ocasiones (Capítulo 7 y 11).

- Seres pesadilla: Se trata de dos plantas que durante el sueño de Corina se transforman en manos y la separan de Mofli (Capítulo 4). Su presencia evidencian la preocupación interna del Sujeto: su miedo a no lograr su Objeto.

3. *Adyuvantes y Oponentes que cambian según la trama:*
- Doctor Fool: Su motivación inicial es divulgar sus conocimientos. No desea hacer mal a al koala pero indirectamente su información provoca que los demás Oponentes conozcan la existencia de Mofli (Capítulo 2) y viajen hasta Australia. Después, al conocer las intenciones genocidas de Mr. Money y sus colaboradores, pasará a ser un claro Adyuvante al enfrentarse al multimillonario.

- Bob Detroit: El narcisista presentador conciencia y divulga en Televisión como Adyuvante sobre los casos de especies que se extinguen (Capítulo 1). También educa al mostrar una imagen de un koala a los espectadores, lo que provoca que Corina descubra que Mofli es el último koala (Capítulo 2). Al mismo tiempo Robert Detroit es Oponente pues al dar la primicia informa sobre la localización concreta del koala dando datos imprescindibles requeridos por los *Oponentes que* aspiran a capturar o matar al pequeño animal (Capítulo 3). Además, el presentador difunde a nivel mundial la recompensa que Mr. Money ofrece a quién le entregue al koala (Capítulo 8).

-   Bruno O'neill: Aunque es amigo de Corina la trata con cierto desdén, especialmente tras la llegada de la nieta de Mr. Money. Actúa como *Oponente* al revelar a Rebeca que Mofli está en las Rocas Blancas (Capítulo 13). Finalmente, Bruno pasa a ser *Adyudante* al salvar al koala engañando a todos pues les hace creer que el koala ha sido devorado por los cocodrilos. Cuando pasa el peligro, Bruno hace entrega a Corina de su amado koala (Capítulo 13). Corina (*Sujeto*) logra su *Objeto*.

4.2. Resultados sobre comparativa del argumento con la Declaración Universal de los Derechos del Animal (1977)

Artículo 1. Todos los animales nacen iguales ante la vida y tienen los mismos derechos a la existencia.

Referido a la igualdad y centrándonos en la trama no todos los animales reciben el mismo tratamiento. La mayoría se presentan como inofensivos salvo otros más agresivos como el diablo de tasmania, único depredador que actúa como *Oponente* al atacar a Mofli (Capítulo 7 y 11). Su actitud violenta se justifica si tenemos en cuenta que representa como otros animales también pueden ser un peligro para los animales en riesgo de extinción, evitando así que el humano figure como único responsable. También los cocodrilos se muestran agresivos aunque estos lo son solo contra otros *Oponentes*, concretamente con Trombonetti y a Paolo (Capítulo 11 y 12). Lo mismo ocurre con el león de África, quien con su zarpazo provoca la cicatriz del rostro de otro *Oponente*: Iván (Capítulo 7).

Artículo 2. a) Todo animal tiene derecho al respeto.

La serie promueve respetar a los animales desde varias perspectivas. Una de ellas el propio diseño de la personalidad del koala y el sentimiento que despierta en la protagonista. Corina lo define de la siguiente manera: "Es como un dulce y perezoso osito de juguete que está vivo y que huele a eucalipto". (Capítulo 4). El *Sujeto* nos hace cómplice de su amor cuando explica a su padre que el propio nombre de "Mofli" se lo dio por sus mofletes: "Sí, parece un bebé glotón de tanto comer eucalipto. ¡Mofletudo! Por eso es Mofli" (Capítulo 6). El mismo principio sugieren sus actos y su relación afectiva cuando juega con el koala (Capítulo 3) aunque, positivamente, no solo él despierta la admiración de Corina. Ella se entusiasma descubriendo especies autóctonas: "¡Mira! Un lorito de cabeza azul" (Capítulo 4); y es capaz de entender a la mariposa Stela (Capítulo 9, Capítulo 10 y Capítulo 11). También es cariñosa con el canguro enano cuando este le ayuda a buscar a Mofli (Capítulo 12).

En contraposición al concepto de respeto encontramos el desinterés inicial de Bruno: "¡Bah! ¡Un pájaro! Tú solo piensas en bichos y pajarracos" (Capítulo 3); o el menosprecio de los *Oponentes*. En este sentido destacan los comentarios que hace Rebeca al hablar de los animales: "¡Bah! El oso panda es un animal muy vulgar" (ídem).

Figura 5: Risa maléfica de Rebeca. (González y Amorós, 1987: Capítulo 12)

Artículo 2. b) El hombre, en tanto que especie animal, no puede atribuirse el derecho de exterminar a los otros animales o de explotarlos violando ese derecho. Tiene la obligación de poner sus conocimientos al servicio de los animales.

El exterminio es uno de los pilares de conducta de los villanos en la serie. Mr. Money se atribuye el derecho a exterminar a los animales en base a su afán de coleccionista y educa a Rebeca en repetir la misma conducta. Por otra parte, sobre la referencia a "los conocimientos al servicio de los animales", el Doctor Fool se preocupa inicialmente más por comunicar sus conocimientos al mundo que de usarlos en beneficio de Mofli. Esta crítica a la vanidad del científico resulta positiva para evidenciar conflictos más sutiles aunque igualmente reales. Finalmente el Doctor Fool, consciente de su error, priorizará el hecho de salvar al koala.

Artículo 2. c) Todos los animales tienen derecho a la atención, a los cuidados y a la protección del hombre.

No existe en los distintos episodios una representación concreta de la figura del veterinario pero sí existe una actitud protectora en Corina y sus *Ayudantes*.

Artículo 3. a) Ningún animal será sometido a malos tratos ni a actos de crueldad.

En *Mofli, el último koala* se rechaza imitar dichas conductas agresivas. Por ello, cuando Paolo golpea a una víbora pensando que se trata de un palo, la víbora es representada como la víctima y él como el agresor (Capítulo 4). Un rechazo más vehemente se produce cuando Paolo golpea a Stela por interponerse mientras trata de capturar a Mofli (Capítulo 10). Igualmente, la serie rechaza el maltrato a los animales depredadores en el momento que el diablo de tasmania es golpeado por Iván y Bailosolo (Capítulo 11) pues, en tal situación, el depredador también es víctima de los mismos *Oponentes* que el koala.

Artículo 3. b) Si es necesaria la muerte de un animal, ésta debe ser instantánea, indolora y no generadora de angustia.

Esta sección no aparece representada.

Artículo 4. a) Todo animal perteneciente a una especie salvaje, tiene derecho a vivir libre en su propio ambiente natural, terrestre, aéreo o acuático y a reproducirse.

El discurso narrativo defiende la libertad del animal salvaje. Por este motivo el *Objeto* de Corina es que Mofli viva libre. Llevarlo a su casa es tan solo una medida temporal hasta que pase el peligro: "No volverás al viejo eucalipto hasta que se hayan ido todos de Rivermint." [...] (Capítulo 9).

Artículo 4. b) Toda privación de libertad, incluso aquella que tenga fines educativos, es contraria a este derecho.

El guion rebate claramente la idea de llevarse a Mofli de su hábitat indistintamente de si la finalidad es científica o con fines lucrativos como el circo de Trombonetti.

Artículo 5. a) Todo animal perteneciente a una especie que viva tradicionalmente en el entorno del hombre, tiene derecho a vivir y crecer al ritmo y en las condiciones de vida y de libertad que sean propias de su especie. b) Toda modificación de dicho ritmo o dichas condiciones que fuera impuesta por el hombre con fines mercantiles, es contraria a dicho derecho.

Este artículo no aparece representado.

Artículo 6. a) Todo animal que el hombre ha escogido como compañero tiene derecho a que la duración de su vida sea conforme a su longevidad natural.

Esta sección no aparece representada.

Artículo 6. b) El abandono de un animal es un acto cruel y degradante.

El abandono animal solo se plantea en una ocasión en el conjunto de la historia durante un diálogo entre Corina y Bailosolo. Sin embargo, la secuencia es un punto de giro ya que en esta conversación la chica cambiará la percepción que tiene de su amigo Bailosolo, intuyendo que su mentalidad es más propia de sus *Oponentes*.

> CORINA: ¿Y qué pasó con tu chimpancé? ¿No te lo quitó nadie, verdad?
>
> BAILOSOLO: ¡No! Lo cambié por un montón de gaseosas.
>
> CORINA: ¡Oh! [...]
>
> CORINA (aparte): Yo no te cambiaré por nada. Nadie te separará de mí.
>
> BAILOSOLO: ¿Y sabes otra cosa?
>
> Corina deja de mirar por la ventana y sale de la casa sin oír más historias de Bailosolo. (González y Amorós, 1987: Capítulo 5)

Artículo 7. Todo animal de trabajo tiene derecho a una limitación razonable del tiempo e intensidad del trabajo, a una alimentación reparadora y al reposo.

Podemos de decir que este Artículo 7 no se presenta como tema o subtema debido a que el único *animal de trabajo* representado en Mofli es un caballo que tira de un coche de caballos (Capítulo 4) sin que se muestre explotación concreta ni tampoco un trato positivo contra la explotación.

Artículo 8. a) La experimentación animal que implique un sufrimiento físico o psicológico es incompatible con los derechos del animal, tanto si se trata de experimentos médicos, científicos, comerciales, como toda otra forma de experimentación. b) Las técnicas alternativas deben ser utilizadas y desarrolladas.

Este artículo no aparece representado.

Artículo 9. Cuando un animal es criado para la alimentación debe ser nutrido, instalado y transportado, así como sacrificado, sin que de ello resulte para él motivo de ansiedad o dolor.

Este artículo no aparece representado.

Artículo 10. a) Ningún animal debe ser explotado para esparcimiento del hombre. b) Las exhibiciones de animales y los espectáculos que se sirvan de animales son incompatibles con la dignidad del animal.

La explotación como pasatiempo no se ofrece visualmente al espectador pero, como ya mencionamos en el artículo 4 sección b, esta acción es repudiada en la trama gracias al tratamiento como *Oponentes* que reciben los circenses de Trombonetti y Paolo. Si bien resulta implícito en el discurso, lo cierto es que no figuran críticas directas a fiestas, exhibiciones o espectáculos de esta índole.

Artículo 11. Todo acto que implique la muerte de un animal sin necesidad es un biocidio, es decir, un crimen contra la vida.

Artículo 12. a) Todo acto que implique la muerte de un gran número de animales salvajes es un genocidio, es decir, un crimen contra la especie.

Para analizar ambos artículos sobre los *biocidios* (Art. 11) y *genocidios* (Art. 12, sección a) hay que tener en cuenta que, tanto en los intentos de matar a Mofli como en los intentos de matar a Stela –u otras mariposas–

, hablamos de intentos de *genocidio* pues Mr. Money o Rebeca son coleccionistas de gran número de animales disecados.

> CORINA: A mí también me gustan las mariposas, sobre todo una.

> REBECA: ¿Una? ¡Bah! En París tengo cientos disecadas.

> CORINA: ¡Ah! ¡¿Entonces las matas?!

> REBECA: ¡Claro! Tampoco voy a disecarlas vivas. (González y Amorós, 1987: Capítulo 10)

Un ejemplo visual del *genocidio* se aprecia durante la presentación de Mr. Money, Rebeca e Iván (Capítulo 1). Durante su encuentro en el salón, observamos que las paredes del multimillonario están decoradas con gran cantidad de cabezas y cuerpos de animales disecados.

> BOB DETROIT: [...] Cada vez van quedando menos animales en el mundo.

> MR. MONEY: ¡No importa! ¡Yo los tengo todos! (ídem)

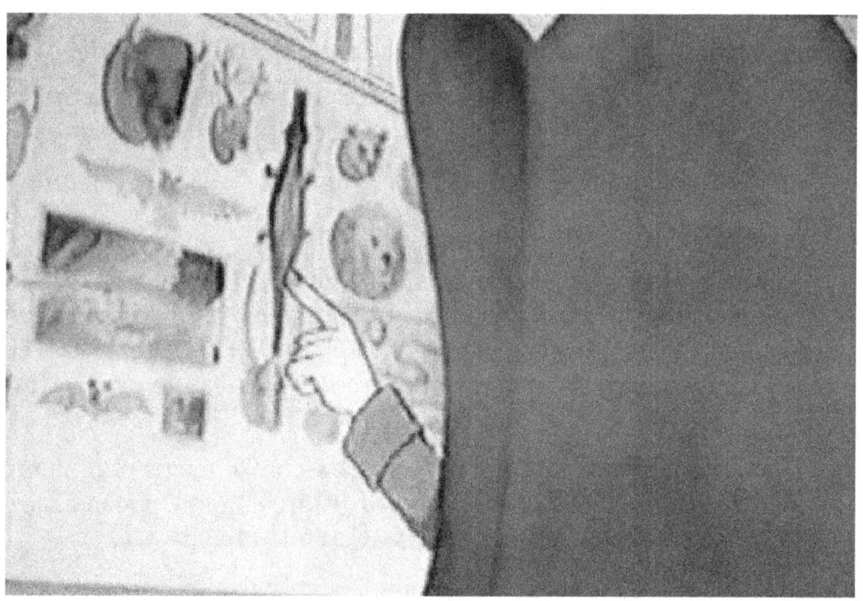

Figura 6: Mr. Money contempla su colección en el Capítulo 1 (González y Amorós, 1987)

Iván es la mano ejecutora del multimillonario y su nieta. Al aparecer por primera vez en el salón de la casa de Mr. Money hace entrega de la cabeza de panda que ha cazado en China (ídem). Si a este ejemplo le sumamos los intentos de matar a Mofli o a Stela, no hay lugar a duda, los *Oponentes genocidas* son los más repudiados por el discurso narrativo. A ellos también se sumará Bailosolo por el interés que le suscita la recompensa que ofrece Mr. Money: "[...] ella misma dulcemente pondrá el koala y la recompensa en nuestras manos" (Capítulo 11).

En general, más allá de los *Oponentes genocidas*, la especie humana se intuye despreocupada ante la extinción de los animales.

> BOB DETROIT: [...] Han desaparecido las ballenas; las focas; continúa el exterminio de algunos felinos... y como todos sabemos hace más de diez años que se extinguieron los koalas. (González y Amorós, 1987: Capítulo 1)

Artículo 12. b) La contaminación y la destrucción del ambiente natural conducen al genocidio.

El contexto de Mofli plantea un mundo inhóspito para los animales ya que el hábitat se reduce a espacios limitados mientras "el mundo ha ido quedándose viejo" (Capítulo 1). En este sentido hay varios ejemplos visuales que plasman el destino de la sociedad que propone la serie:

- Ausencia de árboles en las ciudades: un grupo de perros corren desesperados a orinar en el único árbol visible en la zona. (ídem)

- Torre Eiffel: aparece cubierta de antenas parabólicas. (ídem)

- Las turbogóndolas:

- NARRADOR (OFF): [...] es mediodía en Venecia, Italia. Aquí han cambiado algunas cosas en los últimos años. El ruido, la contaminación, ya no hay palomas en la plaza de San Marcos. Con el tiempo fueron desapareciendo aquellas poéticas góndolas. Hoy solo se ven, ¡Turbogóndolas! (ídem)

- La contaminación también se retrata con la imagen del humo expulsado por el avión ultrasónico de Mr. Money (*Oponentes genocidas*) (Capítulo 3, Capítulo 4 y Capítulo 13).

Por otra parte, el corpus centra más sus esfuerzos en educar en positivo mostrando la naturaleza de Rivermint como un lugar deseable en vez de juzgar la acción destructiva del hombre. Si la ciudad resultaba un lugar desagradable, Rivermint será el hogar de multitud de especies figurantes que dan vida al bosque australiano: águilas, la cacatúa Blanca

–tal vez se trate de la Cacatúa Galerita– (Capítulo 2); salmones (Capítulo 3 y Capítulo 9); un loro de cabeza azul (Capítulo 3); una rana salta de un árbol (Capítulo 10) y también diversos tipos de mariposas en general. Entre los animales figurantes de África también hay cebras (Capítulo 7).

La belleza de la naturaleza se muestra en panorámicas en las que contempla la cascada, el arcoíris, los árboles, etc; e incluso se ensalza, no solo por parte del *Sujeto* o de sus *Adyudantes*, sino también por parte de los *Oponentes* Trombonetti y Paolo:

> TROMBONETTI: ¡Ah! ¡Respira hondo PAOLO! ¡Aquí arriba el aire es más puro! [...]; ¡Mira que maravilla de amanecer, PAOLO! ¡Aplaude, PAOLO! ¡Viva el Sol! ¡Aplaude!
>
> PAOLO: ¡Viva el sol! (González y Amorós, 1987: Capítulo 5)

Los artistas parecen admirar e inspirarse con la naturaleza según expresa el propio del pintor Henk Polhman: "Los pájaros y el aire me traen la inspiración" (Capítulo 6). Su hija, sin embargo, promueve el interés por el el estudio y conocimiento de la fauna:

> BRUNO: ¿De verdad entiendes de flores?
>
> CORINA: Pues claro. Las mimosas parecen de oro y huelen, ¡Mmm! (González y Amorós, 1987: Capítulo 6)

Opuesto a esta defensa de lo natural encontramos la *antítesis* vertida por aquellos que desprecian a la naturaleza. Rebeca es el máximo exponente de estos comentarios. En ellos se asocia el consumismo desmedido y el repudio a la naturaleza:

> REBECA: Discúlpenos Dr. Fool pero con esta oscuridad tan vulgar no le había reconocido. En París todo es luz, y tiendas, boutiques. Pero esta selva... ¡qué pobreza! (González y Amorós, 1987: Capítulo 5)
>
> REBECA: Todas las cataratas son iguales. Agua vulgar y corriente que cae haciendo un ruido desagradable. Le he dicho al abuelo que no me las compre. (González y Amorós, 1987: Capítulo 9)

El discurso narrativo también rechaza que Rebeca destruya las flores por placer (algo cercano a la conciencia del público infantil si tenemos en cuenta que es una acción que está a su alcance rechazar):

> CORINA: ¿Por qué arrancas así las flores?

REBECA: Los pétalos son vulgares. ¡Bah! Me gustan las flores sin flor que huelen sin olor. (González y Amorós, 1987: Capítulo 12)

Artículo 13. a) Un animal muerto debe ser tratado con respeto.

Los únicos animales que aparecen muertos son aquellos que ha disecado Mr. Money a modo de trofeo para su colección. El contexto no transmite que disecar sea respetable con los animales.

Artículo 13. b) Las escenas de violencia en las cuales los animales son víctimas, deben ser prohibidas en el cine y en la televisión, salvo si ellas tienen como fin el dar muestra de los atentados contra los derechos del animal.

Teniendo en cuenta el análisis realizado al conjunto de escenas de violencia en la serie, se confirma que todas estas están justificadas en la producción ya que su finalidad es rehusar dicha agresividad.

Artículo 14. a) Los organismos de protección y salvaguarda de los animales deben ser representados a nivel gubernamental. b) Los derechos del animal deben ser defendidos por la ley, como lo son los derechos del hombre.

Si bien el Artículo 14 no se escenifica literalmente es oportuno citar el siguiente diálogo que invita a proteger a los animales más allá del individualismo y de forma continuada en el tiempo:

CORINA: Mira los peces, Mofli. Ves, nunca dejan de pasar. Cuando desaparece uno tan contento hacia la gran catarata siempre viene otro detrás aún más alegre y bonito. Míralos, Mofli. Pues yo creo que con la vida es igual. El día que yo desaparezca vendrá otra Corina mejor que yo y así siempre. Bueno, siempre no. Dentro de muchísimos años cuando tú desaparezcas ya no habrá otro Mofli tan lindo como tú. Dentro de muchísimos años ya no habrá más koalas en el mundo. (González y Amorós, 1987: Capítulo 9)

5. Discusión y conclusiones.

El mensaje educativo principal de *Mofli, el último koala* (1987) es educar contra el biocidio –especialmente el relativo a la extinción de las especies–. Con este fin se enfatiza el rechazo a los genocidas y a sus ayudantes a la par que se ensalza la representación de la naturaleza como un espacio hermoso que debemos conservar y disfrutar. Además, entre los subtemas relativos a los derechos de los animales destaca la defensa de la libertad de las especies salvajes, representando como *Oponentes* a los intereses comerciales del circo de animales, al turismo masificado y a los propios investigadores que, pese a sus fines educativos, pretendan apartar a los animales de su entorno natural. La serie también es crítica con el progreso globalizado, el consumismo desmedido y la evolución tecnológica contaminante pues la narrativa sugiere que todo ello nos deshumaniza hasta el punto de despreocuparnos por el medioambiente y la vida animal.

Para lograr transmitir este mensaje la historia aplica el distanciamiento a futuro, lo que ayuda a concebir el desastre como un destino evitable si se reacciona a tiempo. Desde el punto de vista empático el recurso principal lo encontramos en el énfasis existente en resaltar la personalidad entrañable del koala y el amor salvador que Corina siente por él. Gracias a esta elección Mofli logra conectar con los espectadores y espectadoras haciendo que el mensaje educativo no solo sea emitido y entendido, sino también sentido.

Otra estrategia importante del guion para conseguir que los más reticentes a lo meloso aprendan la lección la encontramos en la evolución de Bruno. Sus sentimientos muestran el conflicto interno más importante de la historia ya que, como pre-adolescente, se debate entre el niño que era –lo que se asocia a Corina–, o madurar y ser como Rebeca –confundiendo madurar con ser frío y distante–. El conflicto del chico se resuelve cuando, en el último capítulo, él mismo se encarga de salvar al koala de los villanos. Así, su acción muestra que madurará conservando su esencia y favoreciendo la sensación de esperanza del espectador pues le invita a seguir su criterio rechazando el desapego emocional de Rebeca.

Como moraleja, esta elección de Bruno supone que para alcanzar una mejoría social no solo se depende de corazones puros como el de Corina, sino también de aquellos que puedan tardar algo más de tiempo en tomar conciencia en esta cuestión.

Actualmente han transcurrido treinta años de este estreno y, si bien estos valores pudieran resultar ideológicos o irrelevantes para algunos espectadores, debemos tener en cuenta que la extinción de las especies sigue siendo una realidad:

> WWF-Australia calcula que quedan menos de 20.000 koalas en Nueva Gales del Sur y con las actuales tasas, estamos en camino de que se extingan en este estado en 2050", ha dicho el portavoz de la organización, Stuart Blanch, en un comunicado. (EFEVERDE, 2018)

Pese al triste parentesco con el contexto de la serie esperemos que nunca exista "el último koala" y solo sea una de muchas ficciones que conciencien sobre estos valores.

Dicho esto nos despedimos a modo de homenaje con el cierre del guion de Jaime González:

> BOB DETROIT: Alegres y juguetones con su perezosa y confiada amistad. Sin hacer daño a nadie –como diminutos glotones que únicamente buscan brotes y hojas de eucaliptos en un mismo sitio para ser felices–. Ahora ya saben porque no pueden desaparecer los koalas. Si Mofli el último koala se extinguiese, ¿qué ocurriría? Desaparecería el amor. Y el amor, el cariño, la poesía, la sonrisa, la ternura, no pueden desaparecer jamás o todo habrá terminado. ¿Quién de todos los seres vivos? ¿Cuál es el que merece permanecer en todos los corazones? ¡El insustituible! ¡El inapreciable tesoro de la humanidad! ¡El inconmensurable y valioso talismán! ¡El símbolo de la bondad, el cariño y la simpatía! ¡Sí! ¡Sí, amigos! ¡Ese ser único, singular e incomparable tiene un nombre! Y voy a decirlo. Ese ser es... Mofli. (González y Amorós, 1987: Capítulo 13)

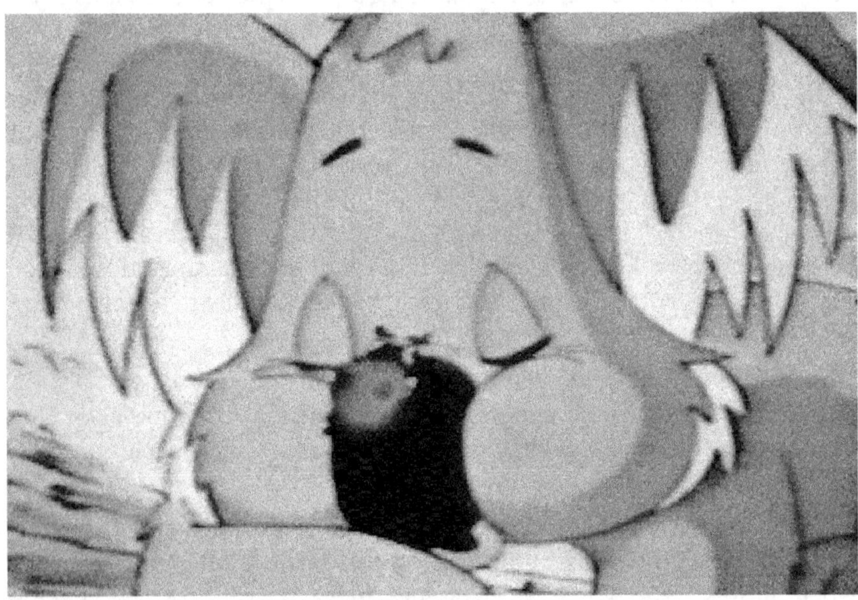

Figura 7: Mofli libre en la última imagen de la serie (González y Amorós, 1987: Capítulo 13)

Referencias bibliográficas

Calvo, S. y Gutiérrez, J. (2007). El espejismo de la educación ambiental, Madrid: Ediciones Morata.

González, J. (Guionista) y Amorós, J. (Director). (1987). Capítulo 1: Rivermint, Capítulo 2: Mofli, Capítulo 3: Llegan los villanos, Capítulo 4: El sueño de Corina, Capítulo 5: El OVNI, Capítulo 6: El heroísmo de Stela, Capítulo 7: El boomerang de Bruno, Capítulo 8: Una carrera alucinante, Capítulo 9: Estalla la tormenta, Capítulo 10: Hipnosis, Capítulo 11: Mofli encuentra un amigo, Capítulo 12: La gran emboscada, Capítulo 13: El fin del principio [Capítulos de serie de televisión]. En Carafí, A. (Productor), Mofli, el último koala. Barcelona: Televisión Española y Equip Studio de Animación.

Greimas, A. J. (1966). Sémantique structurale, París: Larousse (Semántica estructural trad. español De La Fuente Alfredo, Madrid: Gredos, 1987, 3ª ed)

Jiménez Sánchez, A. (2015). El papel o el rol de la mujer en series de animación infantil emitidas en España en el siglo XX y principios del XXI. (Tesis doctora, Universidad Pontificia de Salamanca). Recuperado de https://gredos.usal.es/jspui/handle/10366/127412

Pavis, P. (1998). Dictionarie du théâtre, París: Dunod (Diccionario del teatro trad. español Melendres Jaume, Barcelona: Paidos, 2015, 9ª ed).

Pérez, J. R. (16 enero, 1987). TVE audita y rechaza la producción de dibujos animados 'Mofli, el último koala', El País. Recuperado de https://elpais.com/diario/1987/01/16/radiotv/537750003_850215.html

Román, N. (2007). El modelo actancial y su aplicación, México: Pax México.

Yébenes Cortés, P., Mesonero Izquierdo, R., Rodríguez Díaz, J. A., Viñolo Locubiche, S. (2016). 100 años de animación española, arte y tecnología. Badajoz: Sygnatia.

EFEVERDE (10 octubre, 2018). Los koalas pueden desaparecer en tres décadas por la tala de árboles en el este de Australia. RTVE.es. Recuperado de http://www.rtve.es/noticias/20180910/koalas-pueden-desaparecer-tres-decadas-tala-arboles-este-australia/1795361.shtml

EL PENSAMIENTO FILOSÓFICO DE CERVANTES ENTRE ÉTICA Y ESTÉTICA
(CON MUDANZAS Y VARIACIONES DE ZARABANDA Y CHACONA)

Dr. Francisco Javier Escobar Borrego
Prof. Titular de Literatura Española
Depto. de Literatura Española e Hispanoamericana
Facultad de Filología
Universidad de Sevilla

Resumen

El presente estudio ofrece un análisis de la pervivencia de señeros modelos de la Antigüedad clásica (Apuleyo, Luciano, Séneca, Juvenal y Esopo) en el pensamiento filosófico-literario de Cervantes a partir de *El Quijote* y *El coloquio de los perros*. Para ello me he servido metodológicamente del comparatismo interdisciplinar y la tradición clásica con el objeto de extraer de estas fuentes datos sobre ética y estética, con *mudanzas* y *variaciones* de zarabanda y chacona. Entre los resultados más notables respecto al estado de la cuestión, destaco la sutil hibridación de Cervantes entre Apuleyo y Luciano, autores ambos de una versión dedicada a la metamorfosis del personaje de Lucio en asno, así *El Asno de oro* y *Lucio* o *El asno*, respectivamente, con un toque de magia y hechicería de fondo. Por último, he de resaltar la lectura atenta por parte de Cervantes de la traducción al castellano de *El Asno de oro* por el arcediano hispalense Diego López de Cortegana, cuya *editio princeps* se publicó en la imprenta de su amigo Jacobo Cromberger en 1513. En dicho texto se menciona el término *quijote* que habría de preludiar, en fin, el título de la universal novela de Cervantes.

Palabras clave

Cervantes – El Quijote – El coloquio de los perros – Apuleyo – Luciano

THE PHILOSOPHICAL THOUGHT OF CERVANTES BETWEEN ETHICS AND AESTHETICS (WITH MOVEMENTS AND VARIATIONS OF ZARABANDA AND CHACONA)

Abstract

The present study offers an analysis of the survival of outstanding models of classical antiquity (Apuleius, Lucian, Seneca, Juvenal and Aesop) in the philosophical-literary thought of Cervantes from *Don Quijote* and *El coloquio de los perros*. For this I have served methodologically of interdisciplinary comparatism and the classical tradition in order to extract from these sources data on ethics and aesthetics, with *movements* and *variations* of zarabanda and chacona. Among the most remarkable results regarding the state of the matter, I highlight the subtle hybridization on the part of Cervantes between Apuleius and Lucian, both authors of a version dedicated to the metamorphosis of the character of Lucio in donkey, as well as *El Asno de oro* and *Lucio o El asno*, respectively, with a touch of magic and sorcery in the background. Finally, I must emphasize the careful reading by Cervantes of the translation into Spanish of *El Asno de Oro* by the Archdeacon of Seville, Diego López de Cortegana, whose *editio princeps* was published in the printing press of his friend Jacobo Cromberger in 1513. In this text the term *quijote* is mentioned that would have to prelude, finally, the title of the universal novel by Cervantes.

Key words

Cervantes – El Quijote – El coloquio de los perros – Apuleius – Lucian

1. *Rebuzne el pícaro* o *vida* de perros: el pensamiento filosófico de Cervantes y los arquetipos de la novela antigua

Bien conocida es, en la conformación y forja de la poética narrativa cervantina, la armonización que practicó D. Miguel entre tradición clásica, pensamiento filosófico y novela antigua, en la que Apuleyo ocupó un lugar preeminente entre sus modelos predilectos. Basta recordar *El coloquio de los perros*, en diálogo con *El casamiento engañoso* como historia marco, recurso muy apuleyano por cierto, para comprobarlo: "*Novela y coloquio que pasó entre Cipión y Berganza, perros del hospital de la Resurrección, que está en la ciudad de Valladolid, fuera de la puerta del Campo, a quien comúnmente llaman los perros de Mahúdes*"[18].

Como se ve, más allá de que Berganza constituya seguramente el *alter ego* de Cervantes como autor *caché* u *oculto*, y Cipión, en recuerdo a Escipión, el crítico, resulta clara la hibridación entre la novela dialógica y el coloquio de tradición erasmiana, en entronque con la tradición lucianesca, apuleyana y platónica. No obstante, de Platón bebe también Apuleyo, relacionado a su vez, por la historia del asno, con el cínico Luciano[19], según se indica en el argumento del séptimo libro de *El Asno de oro*, romanceado por el arcediano hispalense Diego López de Cortegana[20], que leyeron Cervantes, Góngora, Lope de Vega y otros ingenios áureos[21].

Pues bien, otra de las modalidades genéricas que Cervantes tuvo en cuenta a partir de su granado conocimiento de la tradición clásica y el pensamiento filosófico viene dado por la *vida* como género literario, con resonancias de Plutarco[22] pero siguiendo la senda conceptual desde las *vidas* de hombres ilustres de Petrarca, escritas a partir de 1337 y brindadas a Francesco da Carrara, hasta obras señeras del humanismo europeo ulterior como el *Elogio de la locura* de Erasmo, con prólogo

---

[18] Cervantes (2010, p. 650). En cuanto al estado de la cuestión, con un selecto panorama crítico: Sáez (2011) y Cárdenas-Rotunno (2016).

[19] Me he servido de las siguientes ediciones: Luciano (1998, 2013).

[20] La *editio princeps* de la traslación al castellano de *El Asno de oro* se publicó en 1513 en la sevillana imprenta de Jacobo Cromberger. Sobre López de Cortegana y su producción de calado humanístico, en la que se integra *El Asno de oro*: Escobar (2001, 2002, 2003, 2013a, 2013b), así como Escobar, Díez y Rivero (2013).

[21] Citaré por mi edición crítica, para la que he tomado como texto *base* el impreso de 1543 conforme a los ejemplares conservados hasta la fecha (Escobar, en prensa*a*); en uno de ellos debió leer *El Asno de oro* "romanceado" y "moralizado" Cervantes; además, para la *collatio codicum*, he tenido en cuenta las distintas *fontes criticae* procedentes de la transmisión editorial desde la *príncipe*. En cuanto a Luciano, me he servido de las siguientes ediciones: Luciano (1998, 2013).

[22] Sáez (2014, 2015).

dedicado a Tomás Moro y la *vida* de este por Fernando de Herrera, en una tradición que culminará, con el tiempo, en un atento lector de Cervantes y su concepto de *vida* como modalidad genérica: Miguel de Unamuno y su *Vida de Don Quijote y Sancho* (1905).

Sea como fuere, Cervantes se sirvió de esta categoría conceptual hasta el punto de que Berganza llega a relatar su *vida* mientras que Cipión promete narrar la suya, aunque esto no se produzca finalmente, teniendo en cuenta además estilemas que atañen a la autorrepresentación, autorreferencialidad e incluso la marca autorial (*sphragís*), de manera que el propio autor puede intervenir como personaje de ficción en su historia novelada; así desde *El Quijote*, I, 6, o el prólogo de las *Novelas ejemplares* (1613), hasta el *Viaje del Parnaso y Adjunta al Parnaso* (1614), como broche a esta línea conceptual de visible experimentación narrativa.

Pero además, en *El coloquio de los perros*, la tradición clásica, y en concreto la novela antigua, brindaba sugerentes precedentes para la picaresca y estas *vidas de perros*, más allá de la *vida de asno* de Apuleyo; es el caso del *Satiricón* de Petronio, del siglo I d. C., aunque sin repercusión prácticamente en el canon genérico español, salvo una traducción de J. Pellicer (Madrid, 1623) y una tardía edición del banquete de Trimalción de 1664. En cambio, en Italia sí se había difundido ya el *ars narrandi* de Petronio en impresos de 1482, en Milán, y 1499, en Venecia. En cualquier caso, la transformación asociada tanto a perros como a asnos, con el tema picaresco del hambre como denominador común, se encuentra en *El Asno de oro* (VII, 3), al decir de Lucio, al tiempo que la imagen de los perros, aunque en otro contexto, se identifica en esta misma obra, así en II, 1, cuando el protagonista se proponga describir una estatua de Diana acompañada de sus perros que parecían verdaderamente vivos, y también en VIII, 2 o IX, 5, entre otros pasajes destacados. Es más, la metamorfosis vinculada a proteicas formas de animales, aunque sea en apariencia metafórica pero que encubren en realidad la naturaleza humana, la hallamos en *El Asno de oro*, VIII, 3, en el episodio del echacuervos de la diosa Siria; o lo que es lo mismo, estamos ante elementos novelescos entre realidad y ficción procedentes de la novela antigua con los que Cervantes debió experimentar cierta empatía incluso connotativa, como se comprueba en *El Asno de oro*, IV, 2, cuando Lucio se halla en la cueva de los ladrones, por el tema del cautivo y la lesión en el brazo en un contexto bélico en el que se refiere la pérdida de dos capitanes en Boecia.

Ahora bien, en consonancia con esta tradición filosófico-literaria, prima en la forja de la poética narrativa de Cervantes, como es sabido, el principio de verosimilitud conforme al "mostrar con propiedad un desatino", tan característico de la novela antigua y que está asociado al placentero deleite de la diversión en virtud de la parodia *compleja*, como manifiesta Luciano en los primeros compases de su *Historia verdadera*, concretamente en el prólogo. No obstante, el autor "cínico" vuelve a recuperar esta sátira a los filósofos como *leitmotiv* en relatos como *Icaromenipo o Menipo en los cielos*, cuyo protagonista es el cínico Menipo, prefiguración, al fin y al cabo, de otros paralelos cervantinos, con utopía al fondo, identificables en el viaje de Clavileño a las esferas celestes y el sueño de Don Quijote en la cueva de Montesinos, hasta los viajes fabulosos y llenos de peripecias en *El Persiles*, en una épica novelesca en prosa alentada por su *emulación* de Heliodoro pero ya identificable en *El Asno de oro*.

Por tanto, cabe poner de relieve, ya de entrada, que Cervantes viene a maridar para sus *vidas de perros*, o *asnos* según se mire, el apuleyanismo vigente en nuestra tradición literaria de personajes marginales y excluidos de la élite social en obras tan señeras como *La Celestina*, y la pervivencia de Luciano en el humanismo europeo. De hecho, la estela de este último autor de notorio abolengo filosófico-dialogístico arranca hacia 1500, prolongándose hasta 1550 bajo el prisma humanístico canónico de dos avisados y experimentados lectores de Apuleyo, o sea Erasmo y Tomás Moro. Con el tiempo, se produce paulatinamente cierta atenuación de su vigencia entre 1550 y 1600, para por fin revitalizarse entre 1600 y 1650 con una vuelta a la tradición primigenia, contexto en el que se viene a ubicar *El coloquio de los perros*, con énfasis en los sueños hasta culminar con obras tan representativas como los *Sueños* de Francisco de Quevedo. Además, en este marco general, hay que destacar sobre todo las aportaciones de Erasmo y Moro entre 1504 y 1514, con una edición de Luciano, aunque sin la *Historia verdadera* o *Relatos verídicos*, las *Opera omnia* (1538) de Luciano por *Micilo*, esto es, un nombre literario tomado de *El Gallo*, editada en Heidelberg, pero sobre todo el aporte de Poggio Bracciolini en armonía con otras traducciones italianas de mediados de siglo que permitirán el calado lucianesco en el humanismo español, con intérpretes y recreadores de la altura y fuste de Francisco de Enzinas o Juan de Vergara, adscrito al entorno humanístico de Alcalá, al tiempo que la enseñanza de Luciano se hará una constante en la *ratio studiorum* de los jesuitas.

Sea como fuere, lo cierto es que, en consonancia con *El Asno de oro*, asistimos a una armonización entre su "pícaro rebuzno" y la tradición lucianesca, con el pensamiento filosófico de los cínicos de por medio. No obstante, estos filósofos, que sustentaban sus juicios sobre la crítica satírica (*parrasía*), la desfachatez (*anaídeia*) y la indiferencia (*adiaphoría*), fueron objetos de semblanzas biográficas, o sea *vidas* como modalidad genérico-literaria, redactadas por Diógenes Laercio en sus *Vidas y opiniones de los filósofos más ilustres*, o *Vidas de filósofos*[23]. Entre estos ilustres cínicos sobresalieron Antístines, el Perro sencillo, autor de *Acerca de Odiseo y Penélope y el perro* y quien conversaba en el gimnasio de Cynosarges, es decir, del 'Perro blanco'; Diógenes de Sinope, quien se consideraba a sí mismo un perro de los que reciben elogios; Hegesias de Sinope, apodado el Collar de Perro; Crates, el filántropo; Mónimo de Siracusa, Onesícrito de Astipalea, Menipo, Menedemo y Metrocles de Maronea. Con todo, sí hay un filósofo que cabe recordar en particular este es, sin duda, Diógenes el Perro, por su libertina mordacidad de palabra a modo de *parresía*. De hecho, se reconoce retratado en los *Diálogos de los muertos* de Luciano, de tanta influencia en los hermanos Alfonso y Juan de Valdés tras la estela de filiación erasmista, como también los *Diálogos de los dioses*, *Menipo*, *Caronte* y otras obras suyas. Ahora bien, el asno "filósofo", con *vida de perro* y un toque ciertamente "cínico", se encontraba ya en el relato de Apuleyo, en concreto en X, 6, en el episodio, en fin, de las fiestas de Corinto.

2. Nuevos *rebuznos* del pícaro: el *mago* Apuleyo, la *vida* de Lucio y un relato marco

A la vista de lo señalado hasta el momento, cabe advertir que el rebuzno del pícaro cervantino no se limitó a las *Novelas ejemplares*, representadas aquí tanto por *El casamiento engañoso* como por *El coloquio de los perros*, sino que en *El Quijote* Cervantes se decantó por una imitación de Apuleyo más allá de que el término "quijote" se identificase en la versión romanceada por López de Cortegana, en concreto en XI, 2[24]. Me refiero a su diálogo intertextual con *El Asno de oro*, III, 2, en alusión a la "industria", ardid o artificio, y otras resonancias respecto a *El Quijote*, I, 35 a propósito del episodio paródico de los cueros u odres de vino y, claro está, en *Donde se da fin a la novela del "Curioso impertinente"*[25] con paralelos temáticos para con *La viuda valenciana* de Lope de Vega, redactada en el período comprendido entre 1595 y 1600, e impresa en 1620 en la XIV Parte de las *Comedias*, en virtud de la poligénesis y los

---

[23] Laercio (2009).
[24] Ofrecí el dato y mis artículos sobre López de Cortegana a F. López Estrada (2004).
[25] Cervantes (1998, pp. 415-417).

loci communes. Sea como fuere, también en *El Quijote* hallamos las huellas del *mago* Apuleyo, a modo de sutil impregnación, en el *mágico* Cervantes y su mesa de trucos o tropelía[26].

Sin embargo, será *El coloquio de los perros*, en articulación narrativa con *El casamiento engañoso*, la novela más apuleyana y de aliento lucianesco de Cervantes, y a la que le otorgó un tratamiento verdaderamente de realce y calado estético. Así, en cuanto a la *dispositio* de las *Novelas ejemplares* como colección o conjunto de historias o cuentos, según recuerda Cervantes en la carta-dedicatoria al Conde de Lemos, *El coloquio de los perros* constituye la coda, en calidad de remate musical polifónico. Es más, en lo que hace a la poliédrica narración de historias teniendo en cuenta un relato marco, como el que proporciona *El casamiento engañoso*, sobresale en *El Asno de oro* la que una *anus*, o anciana, relata a la joven Cárite, tras haber sido raptada por los ladrones de la cueva. De hecho, esta *anilis fabula* se trata del cuento, novela o fábula de Psique y Cupido, que dejó su impronta en *El Persiles*, cuya modulación como relato marco se localiza al final de IV, 4 y prosigue desde IV, 5.

Pues bien, en este contexto narrativo apuleyano, que asimiló Cervantes, destaca la mención a las "ficciones" o "visiones de los sueños" muy en consonancia con la tradición lucianesca, sobre todo cuando la vieja se dirige a Cárite en su *sermocinatio* o parlamento fingido. Por lo demás, su cierre tiene lugar en los últimos compases de VI, 3, en cuyo colofón se integra de nuevo la narración de Lucio al modo autobiográfico. En otras palabras, estamos ante una técnica de novela marco similar a la que se halla entre *El casamiento engañoso* y *El coloquio de los perros* hasta el punto de que finaliza su historia o "conseja" la vieja con el subtema de las bodas de Psique, ya inmortal, y Cupido, o sea, prefiguración *in nuce* de las bodas tanto de Ruperta y Croriano como de Periandro y Auristela en *El Persiles*[27], en un banquete en el que llegan a participar al unísono y en concordia los dioses, humanizados y pertrechados de sus instrumentos musicales, en un *concilium deorum*. Luego proseguirá contando su *vida de perros* Lucio pero no sin antes lamentar no tener a mano tinta y papel para dejar escrita la historia que había escuchado oralmente. De hecho, esta necesidad por parte de Lucio de dejar constancia por escrito de los relatos escuchados y sus distintas versiones se encuentra en otros pasajes de *El Asno de oro*; así, en el cierre de X, 1, en el que el protagonista manifiesta que, más allá de la *cortedad del decir*,

---

[26] Sobre este planteamiento conceptual en virtud de la "metamorfosis" como categoría conceptual: Vivar (2016).
[27] Escobar (2007, 2008).

ha hecho lo posible por transcribir en el libro de su picaresca *vida* todo lo que pudo oír, esto es, de forma similar al *modus operandi* de Campuzano y su conciencia de dejar por escrito la experiencia vivida respecto al *Coloquio* "perruno" en su *curioso* y un tanto *impertinente* cartapacio.

Asimismo, en los episodios cervantinos que tejen la *vida de perros* del filósofo Berganza, otro marco literario destacado de transición que prepara la historia medular de la bruja resulta ser el del atambor[28], habida cuenta de que vincula el personaje de Berganza, es decir el perro sabio, a Cañizares. No obstante, en dicho contexto reticular, los rufianes hurtan al perro sabio[29], como también es hurtado el asno Lucio, incluyendo el símbolo humorístico de la cola que recuerda las controvertidas implicaciones temáticas en *El Quijote* respecto a Sancho y Ginés de Pasamonte, con yerros cervantinos de por medio, en un paralelo respecto a otro gran lector de Apuleyo en el marco humanístico europeo, esto es, François Rabelais y sus *vidas picarescas*, con gigantes en calidad de protagonistas y parodia añadida de los libros de caballerías, en *Gargantúa* y *Pantagruel*.

Sea como fuere, Cervantes vuelve a recrear este *leitmotiv* en *El coloquio* cuando Berganza relate la *vida* de los gitanos al hilo del asno rabón[30], con *loci communes* al tiempo para con los preliminares de López de Cortegana y Juan de Tovar en *El Asno de oro*. Tanto es así que el propio Berganza manifiesta asemejarse figuradamente a un asno, de manera que, al recordar a su amo poeta o autor de comedias, cuyo talento era merecedor del manteo como castigo, o sea como le sucedió a Sancho Panza, viene a sintetizar la narración de esta experiencia iniciática y la de otros amos, es decir, "en figuras fingidas y en bellezas de artificio y de transformación"[31].

Por tanto, asistimos a una *exhaustio* narrativa en la *vida de perros* del filósofo Berganza por parte de Cervantes, con implicaciones estéticas respecto a la trama de *El casamiento engañoso* en lo que hace al simbólico Hospital de la Resurreción, evocado bien a cuento a propósito de estas "metamorfosis" y de "regreso" a la vida, como le habrá de suceder también a Campuzano. En cualquier caso, en dicho marco contextual, la referencia al día, en contraste respecto a la noche como límite temporal del coloquio entre los dos perros hermanos y filósofos, viene a

---

[28] Cervantes (2010, pp. 694 ss.).
[29] Cervantes (2010, pp. 695-696).
[30] Cervantes (2010, pp. 720-721).
[31] Cervantes (2010, pp. 727-730).

constituir un *leitmotiv*[32] hasta el punto de que marca el cierre de *El coloquio*, en un nuevo contrapunto entre el día y la noche, como apostilla Cipión al hilo de "arrimarse al árbol" de los amos, tan arraigado en la tradición picaresca, con la intención frustrada de contar su *vida de perros*[33]. En fin, la noche articula y modula con frecuencia los diferentes cuentos y acciones urdidos en la trama narrativa[34], con las palabras del alférez Campuzano a su interlocutor Peralta de fondo[35].

Ahora bien, la necesidad de establecer un pacto de confianza con el interlocutor por parte de quien relata tan *fabulosa* historia, recurso muy cervantino por cierto, se localiza ya en *El Asno de oro*, I, 1, en concreto cuando uno de los caminantes con los que se encuentra Lucio, es decir Aristómenes, le ruega a este que dé firme crédito a los episodios de magia de los que fue objeto su amigo Sócrates. De hecho, este último llega a enumerar la amplia aretalogía de la maga, entre la que se halla, claro está, "metamorfosear" los hombres en naturaleza animal; o lo que es lo mismo, en un episodio de magia que se desarrolla en el capítulo II del libro I, según se indica en el argumento, en correspondencia con la focalización en la *vida* de perros desde la perspectiva narrativa de Campuzano[36], mientras que Peralta no puede dar credibilidad a la fabulosa y *disparatada* narración de su amigo[37], a lo que le habrá de responder finalmente Campuzano con vistas a cumplir el principio narrativo de verosimilitud de Cervantes como autor *caché*[38].

Se trata, en fin, de una remota tradición literaria que conlleva por añadidura la vuelta del "tiempo de Maricastaña" para "estos varones sabios", según prosigue Campuzano[39], en armonía con otras huellas de la tradición clásica que van desde la sátira de Séneca en el *Apocolocyntosis*, esto es, uno de los textos más difundidos a principios del siglo XVII con resonancias en Diego de Velázquez y su representación pictórica del

---

[32] Cervantes (2010, pp. 734-735).

[33] Cervantes (2010, p. 736).

[34] Cervantes (2010, p. 736).

[35] Cervantes (2010, p. 643).

[36] Cervantes (2010, p. 644).

[37] Cervantes (2010, p. 644).

[38] Cervantes (2010, p. 645).

[39] En virtud de las siguientes palabras: "Las cosas de que trataron fueron grandes y diferentes, y más para ser tratadas por varones sabios que para ser dichas por bocas de perros. Así que, pues yo no las pude inventar de mío, a mi pesar y contra mi opinión, vengo a creer que no soñaba, y que los perros hablaban.
-¡Cuerpo de mí! –replicó el licenciado–. Si se nos ha vuelto el tiempo de Maricastaña, cuando hablaban las calabazas, o el de Isopo, cuando departía el gallo con la zorra y unos animales con otros." (Cervantes: 2010, p. 645).

bufón Juan Calabazas o Calabacillas (1639), el aliento de Isopo o "Guiso-
pete" en *Quijote*, II, 27, con la edición sevillana de Esopo por el humanista Diego Girón[40], pero especialmente en entronque con la tradición
lucianesca, así en el *Icaromenipo*, que tiene como protagonista al cínico
Menipo. No obstante, en el relato, en un sabroso diálogo entre la Luna
y el cínico Menipo, que incluye el contraste contrapuntístico entre el
fulgor lumínico y la noche, se identifica cierta retórica del silencio[41],
aplicada a los hechos vergonzantes de los filósofos, y en oposición a la
virtud defendida por Cervantes en estas *vidas de perros* y hasta en su
propio retrato como autor-personaje en el *Viaje del Parnaso*, tanto por
sus lenguas indiscretas como por sus pasiones humanas y mundanas.

Pues bien, en lo que al relato lucianesco se refiere, más adelante se llega
a identificar una nueva sátira caricaturesca de los murmuradores filósofos y su pretendida virtud mediante máscaras y túnica de oro en el
mismo relato en la voz de Zeus y su convocatoria de asamblea adivina a
petición de la Luna, esto es, en contraste respecto a la capa modesta de
la virtud con la que Cervantes resulta ser canonizado por Apolo en el
Viaje del Parnaso, *leitmotiv* que habrá de retomar Berganza cuando relate su vuelta a Sevilla, tras abandonar su anterior oficio de cuidador de
ganado llegando a ser maltratado a palos[42].

En efecto, el motivo o subtema del animal apaleado, como en la *vida de
perros* de Berganza, se encuentra en *El Asno de oro*, III, 5 y reaparece en
IV, 1, marco contextual en el que un mancebo hortelano golpea sin pie-
dad y con acritud al asno Lucio cuando deseaba morder las rosas, a

---

[40] Compañero académico de Fernando de Herrera y Cristóbal Mosquera de Figueroa, este último amigo, a su vez, del escritor alcalaíno.

[41] Consonante, al tiempo, con las reticencias y elipsis narrativas de los pícaros, comenzando
ya, en la tradición española, por Lázaro de Tormes.

[42] En una escena conocida para los *rebuznos del pícaro*: "Como me vi suelto corrí a él, ro-
déele todo, sin osar llegarle con las manos, acordándome de la fábula de Isopo, cuando aquel
asno, tan asno que quiso hacer a su señor las mismas caricias que le hacía una perrilla rega-
lada suya, que le granjearon ser molido a palos. Pareciome que en esta fábula se nos dio a
entender que las gracias y donaires de algunos no están bien en otros; apode el truhán, jue-
gue de manos y voltee el histrión, rebuzne el pícaro, imite el canto de los pájaros y los diversos gestos y acciones de los animales y los hombres el hombre bajo que se hubiere dado a
ello, y no lo quiera hacer el nombre principal, a quien ninguna habilidad destas le puede dar
crédito ni nombre honroso.
CIPIÓN. Basta. Adelante, Berganza, que ya estás entendido.
BERGANZA. ¡Ojalá que, como tú me entiendes, me entendiesen aquellos por quien lo digo! Que
no sé qué tengo de buen natural, que me pesa infinito cuando veo que un caballero se hace
chocarrero y se precia que sabe jugar los cubiletes y las agallas, y que no hay quien como él
sepa bailar la chacona." (Cervantes: 2010, pp. 667-668).

modo de antídoto, para después volver a ser maltratado por los ladrones; es decir, violencia gratuita muy acorde con el género de la picaresca desde el *Lazarillo*, sus continuaciones e imitaciones, pero no ausente ni en *El coloquio de los perros*, ni en *El casamiento engañoso*, como tampoco en *El Quijote* de 1605 y 1615. Estamos, en síntesis, ante un *leitmotiv* muy destacado en otros pasajes de *El Asno de oro* por el tema de la mala fortuna o mudable hado, esencial en esta obra y que Cervantes pudo advertir, por ejemplo en VII, 4.

Por lo demás, en *El coloquio*, junto a estas deudas respecto al apuleyanismo que dejaría su huella en ingenios como Lope de Vega, Góngora o Quevedo, se trata de una fábula atribuida a Esopo, de notoria tradición literaria desde *Zifar*, 33-34 y el *Libro de buen amor*, 1401-1507, al *Esopete ystoriado*, I, 17, como se apunta en *El casamiento engañoso*[43] para volver a aparecer de nuevo en *El coloquio*, en concreto en el episodio marco del atambor, contexto en el que Berganza, en calidad de perro sabio, hace monerías a modo de espectáculo. Para ello Cervantes decidió evocar el baile de la zarabanda y la chacona[44], o sea danzas de inspiración lasciva conforme al decoro de la picaresca pero empleada igualmente por los autores cultos en sus composiciones, así nuestro escritor, como hace también en *La ilustre fregona*, en armonía con las danzas de carácter erótico zarabandas y folías, a propósito de la picaresca sevillana

---

[43] Cervantes (2010, p. 645).
[44] Cervantes (2010, p. 699); para el pensamiento musical del escritor alcalaíno, con un estado de la cuestión: Escobar (2018b).

con la referencia al Compás en un atractivo diálogo entre el Asturiano
y Barrabás[45].

---

[45] Dice así: "-Hermano mozo, contrapás es un baile extranjero, y no motejo de mal vestidos.
-Si eso es –replicó el mozo–, no hay para qué nos metan en dibujos; toquen sus zarabandas,
chaconas y folías al uso, y escudillen como quisieren, que aquí hay personas que les sabrán
llenar las medidas hasta el gollete.
El Asturiano, sin replicar palabra, prosiguió su canto, diciendo:

 Entren, pues, todas las ninfas
 y los ninfos que han de entrar,
que el baile de la chacona
es más ancho que la mar. [...]

Escupan al hideputa
porque nos deje holgar,
puesto que de la chacona
nunca se suele apartar. [...]

El baile de la chacona
encierra la vida bona. [...]

El brío y la ligereza
en los viejos se remoza,
y en los mancebos se ensalza
y sobre modo se entona,
que el baile de la chacona
encierra la vida bona.

¡Qué de veces ha intentado
aquesta noble señora,
con la alegre zarabanda,
el Péseme y Perra mora,

entrarse por los resquicios
de las caras religiosas
a inquietar la honestidad
que en las santas celdas mora!

¡Cuántas fue vituperada
de los mismos que la adoran!
Porque imagina el lascivo
y al que es necio se le antoja

que el baile de la chacona
encierra la vida bona. [...]

Y que sola la chacona
encierra la vida bona." (Cervantes, 2010, pp. 493-496).

Ahora bien, las danzas y monerías de Berganza tienen ya su paralelo en las que había realizado el asno Lucio tras haberle enseñado el criado de un caballero (X, 3), como se pone de manifiesto ya en el argumento, hasta el punto de que las habilidades de Lucio como *asno sabio* cierran, en efecto, el capítulo, con implicaciones narrativas y de desarrollo temático en X, 5 y X, 6, según se comprueba en los respectivos argumentos. En fin, a esta vuelta de los "tiempos pasados" de las fábulas en *El coloquio* se habrá de referir de nuevo el alférez mientras que le hace copartícipe a su interlocutor de que ha transcrito el "coloquio" de los perros[46], lo que viene a agradar a Peralta[47], en tanto que, por su parte, Campuzano le adelanta que lo ha tomado fielmente "de coro"[48].

3. Difícil cosa el no escribir sátiras: *vidas* de perros y contrarcadia pastoril con sabor a parodia

A la vista de lo señalado para *El coloquio*, cabe añadir al análisis propuesto la hibridación genérica por parte de Cervantes de la *tonalidad* picaresca con crítica al idealismo de la ficción pastoril, identificable, una vez más, en *El Asno de oro*, como se comprueba en VII, 4. De hecho, se incluye como materia estética el maltrato al animal, en una contra-arcadia, y la presencia de perros y lobos, o sea, como en el relato de Cervantes[49]. Asimismo, el peligro de los lobos desde la perspectiva del animal que cuenta su *vida*, esto es, Lucio en correspondencia con Berganza, reaparece en El *Asno de oro* a modo de *leitmotiv*, como se ve en VIII, 2, mientras que en el relato de Cervantes sobresale la polionomasia Berganza – Barcino, con una caracterización próxima al comportamiento de un pícaro.

Pues bien, al margen de su color rojizo, como el traidor Judas, Barcino es el nombre de un perro que regala el bachiller Sansón Carrasco a Don Quijote. Además, en este contexto pastoril, un Barcino se menciona en *El pastor de Fílida* (1582) de Luis Gálvez de Montalvo, amigo de Cervantes al tiempo que fautor en la presentación en sociedad de *La Galatea*, cuando esta *sale a la plaza*. Con todo, aunque en este Barcino se ha querido ver por parte de la crítica la ficcionalización o trasunto literario de Jacopo Sannazaro, sin embargo, a mi entender, podría tratarse del

---

46 Cervantes (2010, pp. 645-646).
47 Cervantes (2010, p. 646).
48 Cervantes (2010, p. 646).
49 Cervantes (2010, p. 659).

poeta barcelonés Cariteo, adscrito a este círculo de élite de Sannazaro, Giovanni Pontano y Egidio da Viterbo.

Sea como fuere, en este contexto poliédrico cervantino, se viene a realzar de nuevo la retórica del silencio, esto es, conforme a la más granada tradición del género picaresco, así la reticencia y elipsis narrativas de Lázaro, como se recordará, pero también identificable tanto en los relatos mencionados de Luciano como en *El Asno de oro*. Respecto a esta última obra en particular, se halla en III, 3, en palabras de Andria dirigidas a Lucio, hasta el punto de que constituye un claro *leitmotiv* que retornará un poco más adelante en ese mismo capítulo, cuando Andria vuelva a dialogar con Lucio sobre su *impertinente curiosidad* a la hora de aprender artes mágicas con el objeto de "metamorfosearse" en otra figura. En cualquier caso, en esta modulación híbrida entre las *vidas* de pícaros y pastores se llega a evocar a Juvenal y su Sátira I, 30 ("era difícil cosa el no escribir sátiras")[50]; en otros términos, como en el arranque del autorretrato o *vida* que realiza Cervantes con un toque de *indignación* en el capítulo cuarto del *Viaje del Parnaso* a imitación de Cesare Caporali, si bien más adelante habría de decir en IV, 34-36: "Nunca voló la pluma humilde mía / por la región satírica, baxeza / que a infames premios y desgracias guía"[51]. Como contrapunto, Avellaneda le devolvió otro retrato muy distinto en el que, entre otras lindezas a modo de invectiva *ad hominem* sobre la *vida* y obra de Cervantes, manifestaba que sus *Novelas* eran más "satíricas" que "ejemplares"; tampoco Lope de Vega enalteció demasiado la producción novelística cervantina en el preámbulo, o historia *abreviada* de la novela entre Italia y España, de sus *Novelas a Marcia Leonarda*, dedicadas a Marta de Nevares. En cualquier caso, en el relato cervantino, habrán de primar las sucesivas indicaciones de Cipión para dirigir el *discurso de* la *vida* de Berganza[52], con apunte incluido a Mauleón como personaje de aliento popular, en correspondencia con *Quijote*, II, 71, a la Academia de los Imitadores o Imitatoria, recordada en *Las seiscientas apotegmas* (1596) de Juan Rufo[53], y

---

[50] Esto es: "CIPIÓN. Por haber oído decir que dijo un gran poeta de los antiguos que era difícil cosa el no escribir sátiras, consentiré que murmures un poco de luz y no de sangre; quiero decir que señales y no hieras, ni des mate a ninguno en cosa señalada; que no es buena la murmuración, aunque haga reír a muchos, si mata a uno; y si puedes agradar sin ella, te tendré por muy discreto." (Cervantes, 2010, p. 659).

[51] Cervantes (1991, p. 114).

[52] Cervantes (2010, p. 661).

[53] Escobar (en prensa*b*).

finalmente al acuerdo explícito de no murmurar de nadie, con los filósofos cínicos y su *parresía* satírica al fondo, cuando Berganza refiera sus impagables e ímprobos servicios al mercader en Sevilla[54].

Por lo demás, destacan las fórmulas demarcativas o delimitativas por parte de Cipión ante el discurso autobiográfico de Berganza, tras recordar, en un prolijo excurso, la relación de personajes estereotipados de la tradición pastoril y sus *vidas*[55], como complemento a sus indicaciones por parte de Cipión para dirigir el *cuento de la vida* de Berganza[56], y más adelante, al hilo del estudio de la Compañía de Jesús en Sevilla y con el tema del hambre, tan picaresco, en calidad de *colonna sonora*[57]. Asimismo, también se prepara la narración de un cuento con referencia, una vez más, a Sevilla, llevada a cabo la descripción de la casa y patio de Monipodio[58], en correspondencia especular respecto a *Rinconete y Cortadillo*, teniendo su analogía el motivo de los ladrones que roban un caballo en *El Asno de oro*, III, 5, como se indica ya en el argumento. Además, al hilo del episodio marco o de transición del atambor, Cipión llega a interrumpir la narración de Berganza para que no se queden "a la sombra del silencio"[59], en tanto que la sombra y el silencio vuelven a ser evocados por Cipión cuando Berganza relate su servicio al morisco, quien lo mataba de hambre[60].

Por último, en este contexto intertextual con visibles dosis de sátira e ironía, no falta una historia *abreviada* de las *vidas* pastoriles acompañada de una crítica al exceso de idealización sin conciencia de realidad, desde *La Diana* de Jorge de Montemayor, con el episodio del agua mágica de Felicia como paralelismo respecto a *El Quijote*, I, 6[61], a *La Arcadia* de Lope de Vega, *El pastor de Fílida* de Luis Gálvez de Montalvo, e incluso *La Galatea*[62], como una autorrepresentación o autorreferencialidad afín también al *donoso escrutinio*, con nuevas resonancias más adelante en el *discurso de la vida* de Berganza entre las que no falta la canción popular "cata el lobo do va Juanica", con aires de paremiología entre la voz y la palabra[63].

---

[54] Cervantes (2010, pp. 670-671).

[55] Cervantes (2010, p. 662).

[56] Cervantes (2010, p. 662).

[57] Cervantes (2010, pp. 672-673).

[58] Cervantes (2010, p. 691).

[59] Cervantes (2010, p. 697).

[60] Cervantes (2010, p. 723).

[61] Y otras prefiguraciones cervantinas respecto a su *Arcadia fingida*, *contrahecha* o *pastoral Arcadia*.

[62] Cervantes (2010, pp. 660-661); también Cervantes (2014).

[63] Cervantes (2010, pp. 661-662).

4. Conclusiones, análisis de resultados y perspectivas críticas abiertas

En resumidas cuentas, hemos asistido a sucesivas "metamorfosis" y "transformaciones" desde Apuleyo y Luciano a Cervantes para unas *vidas de perros*, con *asnos* incluidos, en imágenes e instantáneas para la comprensión del imaginario de la *vida* picaresca de la ciudad de Sevilla y de sus protagonistas actantes. Se comprueba especialmente en *El coloquio de los perros*, con una sutil inclinación hacia una etapa de conversión espiritual, en el caso de López de Cortegana, autor de la traducción de *El Asno de oro* que leyó Cervantes, y hasta el mismo autor alcalaíno en los últimos compases de su vida, como le habría de criticar Avellaneda en *El Quijote* apócrifo entre burlas y veras. Como se ha podido comprobar, para el análisis planteado me he servido de categorías conceptuales tales como autorreferencialidad y *autor caché* en un marco de sociabilidad estética, de manera que este proceder técnico circunscrito a la autorrepresentación en el discurso con el objeto de recrear los cambios vitales y avatares existenciales del creador, como en Cervantes o López de Cortegana, constituye un recurrente arquetipo en las estructuras antropológicas del imaginario estético cervantino, esto es, en la *vida* como en el arte. Así lo estaba viviendo nuestro escritor a nivel de experiencia humana, con el apuleyanismo hispalense al fondo, y además lo había leído bajo el arrope de la ficción en modelos canónicos de la Antigüedad clásica; es decir, en las *Metamorfosis* o *El Asno de oro* de Apuleyo, complementarias a las *Metamorfosis* de Ovidio, y en los relatos y diálogos de Luciano, entre la realidad y la ficción, la vigilia y el sueño.

Por ello Cervantes sabía que la *vida* del ser humano, o su representación ficticia en un animal como estos *perros* (*asnos*) filósofos, como también las fábulas esópicas editadas al cuidado del humanista Diego Girón, estaba sujeta a un continuo proceso de cambio e inevitable impermanencia; de hecho, se producía bien en la ficción literaria o en la realidad, como un perenne proceso de búsqueda y crecimiento personal a modo de *perpetuum mobile*. Tanto es así que se materializaba con frecuencia en constantes filosóficas y ontológicas, en calidad de interrogantes para estas *vidas de perros* o *de asnos*, o sea, *sé lo que eres* o *sé lo que quieres ser*, con guiños pindáricos en la tradición literaria clásica hasta la construcción cambiante identitaria de Don Quijote y su *acabamiento* final, y sobre todo en la *resurrección* en el diálogo entre *El casamiento engañoso* y *El coloquio de los perros*, como he puesto de relieve. En el caso de Don Quijote, el ingenioso caballero andante acabará volviendo a su condición de hidalgo, pero con transformación *inmortal* en calidad de leyenda o personaje legendario para la posteridad literaria. En definitiva, queda todavía mucho por decir siguiendo la recta senda de ejemplares *vidas de arte* a la cervantina[64], aunque sean *vidas de perros*, porque, como leyó Cervantes en la traducción de López de Cortegana, todos llevamos a cuesta un asno y no precisamente de oro; algunos incluso de plata, como el *asno de plata* de Juan Ramón Jiménez, gran lector por cierto de Cervantes. Por todo ello, *rebuzne el pícaro*.

---

[64] Al respecto he ofrecido ya un avance en Escobar (2018a).

Referencias bibliográficas

Cárdenas-Rotunno, A. J. (2016). De perros y asnos: Cervantes y la tradición. *Anuario de Estudios Cervantinos*, 12, 199-212.

Cervantes, M. de (1991). *Viaje del Parnaso. Poesías varias*, ed. E. L. Rivers. Madrid: Espasa-Calpe.

____________ (1998). *Don Quijote de la Mancha*, ed. Instituto Cervantes, dir. F. Rico, Barcelona: Instituto Cervantes – Crítica.

____________ (2010). *Novelas ejemplares*, ed. J. García López. Barcelona: Crítica, 2ª ed.

____________ (2014). *La Galatea*, ed. J. Montero, en colaboración con F. J. Escobar y F. Gherardi. Madrid – Barcelona: Real Academia Española – Galaxia Gutenberg – Círculo de Lectores.

Escobar Borrego, F. J. (2001). Textos preliminares y posliminares de la traslación del *Asinus aureus* por Diego López de Cortegana: sobre el planteamiento de la traducción. *Cuadernos de Filología Clásica. Estudios Latinos*, 21, 151-175.

____________ (2002). Diego López de Cortegana traductor del *Asinus aureus*: el cuento de Psique y Cupido. *Cuadernos de Filología Clásica. Estudios Latinos*, 22.1, 193-210.

____________ (2003). Una edición del siglo XVI de hecho desconocida: la traducción del *Asinus aureus* por Diego López de Cortegana (Sevilla, Doménico de Robertis, 1546). *Il Confronto Letterario. Quaderni del Dipartimento di Lingue e Letterature Straniere Moderne dell'Università di Pavia*, 39, 7-14.

____________ (2007). El binomio *Formonsitas / Pulchritudo* en El *Persiles*: de la belleza corpórea a la categoría simbólico-mítica. *Anuario de Estudios Cervantinos. Cervantes entre dos Siglos de Oro: De "La Galatea" al "Persiles"*, 3, 233-256.

____________ (2008). Nuevos datos para la lectura de la historia de Croriano y Ruperta (*Persiles*, III, 17): a vueltas con los aspectos mítico-retóricos. En J. M.ª Maestre *et alii* (eds.), *Humanismo y Pervivencia del Mundo Clásico. Homenaje al profesor Antonio Prieto* (pp. 287-302). Madrid – Alcañiz: CSIC – Instituto de Estudios Humanísticos, vol. IV. 1.

___________ (2013a), Diego López de Cortegana y Erasmo: la traducción de la *Querela Pacis* (Sevilla, Jacobo Cromberger, 1520). En F. J. Escobar, S. Díez y L. Rivero (eds.), *La "metamorfosis" de un inquisidor: el humanista Diego López de Cortegana (1455-1524)*, (pp. 133-163). Sevilla – Huelva: Universidad de Sevilla – Universidad de Huelva – Ayuntamiento de Cortegana.

___________ (2013b), Nuevos datos sobre la versión del *Asno de Oro*, de Diego López de Cortegana: bases para una edición crítica. En M. Bélime-Droguet, V. Gély-Ghédira, L. Mailho-Daboussi y Ph. Vendrix (eds.), *Psyché à la Renaissance* (pp. 75-107). Turnhout: BREPOLS.

___________ (2018a). *Vidas de arte en el Humanismo hispalense. De Nebrija a Góngora*, pról. J. Garau. México: Frente de Afirmación Hispanista, A. C.

___________ (2018b). Resuene el cuento de Silerio: *Psalle et sile* o intersecciones dialogísticas en *La Galatea* (con tres variaciones y rondó final). *E-Spania. Revue interdisciplinaire d'études hispaniques médiévales et modernes*, 29, 1-43.

___________ (en prensaa). *El Asno de oro (Medina del Campo, 1543)*. México: Frente de Afirmación Hispanista, A. C.

___________ (en prensab). *Materiam superabat opus*: Cervantes, *cautivo* lector de Rufo (al trasluz de la modalidad épico-novelesca en *La Austríada* y los *Apotegmas*). *Creneida. Anuario de Literaturas Hispánicas*.

Escobar, F. J., Díez, S. y Rivero. L., eds. (2013). *La "metamorfosis" de un inquisidor: el humanista Diego López de Cortegana (1455-1524)*. Sevilla – Huelva: Universidad de Sevilla – Universidad de Huelva – Ayuntamiento de Cortegana.

Laercio, D. (2009). *Vidas de filósofos cínicos, con La secta del perro de C. García Gual*. Madrid: Alianza Editorial, 3º reimp.

López Estrada, F. (2004). Quixotes en el Apuleyo castellano. En P. Civil (ed.), *Siglos dorados. Homenaje a Augustin Redondo* (pp. 797-805). Madrid: Editorial Castalia, vol. II.

Luciano (1998). *Relatos fantásticos*, introd. C. García Gual. Madrid: Alianza Editorial.

___________ (2013). *Historia verdadera*, trad. F. Socas, ilustr. J. Socas. Sevilla: Ediciones La Piedra lunar.

Sáez, A. J. (2011), El "divino don de la habla": *El coloquio de los perros* desde la tradición clásica y bíblica (contribución al estudio de sus fuentes). En C. Strosetzki (ed.), *Visiones y revisiones cervantinas. Actas selectas del VII Congreso Internacional de la Asociación de Cervantistas. Münster, 30 septiembre- 4 de octubre 2009* (pp. 797-806). Alcalá de Henares: Centro de Estudios Cervantinos.

__________ (2014). Más sobre Cervantes, Plutarco y los cínicos: una anécdota de Alcibíades y *El coloquio de los perros. Anales Cervantinos*, 46, 149-160.

__________ (2015), Ecos y referentes clásicos en *El coloquio de los perros* de Cervantes. En J. M.ª Maestre *et alii* (eds.), *Humanismo y Pervivencia del Mundo Clásico. V.3. Homenaje al profesor Juan Gil* (pp. 2701-2716). Madrid – Alcañiz: CSIC – Instituto de Estudios Humanísticos.

Vivar, F. (2016). El arte de la metamorfosis y el arte de la novela: Apuleyo y Cervantes. *eHumanista. Journal of Iberian Studies*, 33, 318-330.

*Este libro se terminó de elaborar en julio de 2019
en la ciudad de Sevilla, bajo los cuidados de
Francisco Anaya, director de Ediciones Egregius.*